1

2

3

4

EAGLE VALLEY LIB.
P.O. BOX 240   600 BROADWAY
EAGLE, CO 81631   (970) 328-8800

THE SOURDOUGH SCHOOL

Vanessa Kimbell

THE SOURDOUGH SCHOOL

THE GROUNDBREAKING GUIDE TO MAKING GUT-FRIENDLY BREAD

PHOTOGRAPHY BY NASSIMA ROTHACKER

KYLE BOOKS

To my amazing Mother, for teaching a little girl to love baking,
and to my gorgeous Father for always eating everything I ever baked with enthusiasm.

An Hachette UK Company
www.hachette.co.uk

First published in Great Britain in 2018 by
Kyle Books, an imprint of Kyle Cathie Ltd
Carmelite House
50 Victoria Embankment
London EC4Y 0DZ
www.kylebooks.co.uk

This edition published 2018

ISBN 978-1-90948-793-2

Distributed in the US by Hachette Book Group,
1290 Avenue of the Americas, 4th and 5th Floors,
New York, NY 10104

Distributed in Canada by Canadian Manda Group,
664 Annette St., Toronto, Ontario, Canada M6S 2C8

Editors **Vicky Orchard and Judith Hannam**
Editorial Assistant **Isabel Gonzalez-Prendergast**
Americanizing **Lee Faber**
Design **Helen Bratby**
Photography **Nassima Rothacker**
Food styling **Adam Pagor and Vanessa Kimbell**
Cover illustration **Stuart Simpson**
Production **Nic Jones and Gemma John**

Printed and bound in China

10 9 8 7 6 5 4 3 2 1

Note: As baking bread requires precise
measurements, all quantities here are
given in grams.

CONTENTS

Foreword
by Richard Hart

I haven't always been a baker. I started my career in baking at the age of 30, and it quickly became an obsession—an obsession that drove me from never having made a loaf of bread, to being Head Baker at Tartine in a matter of years. Now I have gone on to partner with Noma, and I am in the process of opening my own Hart's Bakeries to share my knowledge and love of sourdough.

I first met Vanessa while still at Tartine, when she came to interview me about sourdough for BBC Radio 4's *Food Programme*. It quickly became clear that Vanessa shared my obsession, and we speak often, talking bread and techniques. We also share a belief that great bread is for everyone.

The art of bread baking takes time, dedication, and practice. You can't just follow a formula; you have to develop an understanding with your bread. Sourdough is a living thing, it's challenging, and requires love and care. It's influenced not only by the environment in which it's made, but where the ingredients are grown, and as a baker you need to pay attention to every detail.

In this book Vanessa gives you the tools you need to be a successful baker. If you take this knowledge and focus, you will be rewarded with beautiful, freshly-baked bread. Making sourdough is addictive, and there is nothing better than pulling a handmade loaf out of the oven.

Making bread using a sourdough starter also gives you better bread. The texture and flavor are far superior to that of a yeasted loaf. Sourdough bread is also fundamentally better for your body. The bacteria in the sourdough help break down the flour, which makes it more digestible and nutritious. Vanessa has a unique understanding of this process, which she shares with you here, and the fact that sourdough bread is more nourishing.

This book is interactive. It shouldn't just be followed like a regular formula book. You should pick it up and read it thoroughly, and use it as a series of steps to help you best understand your own environment and flour. It's not easy. You need to be completely aware of your ingredients and surroundings, to pay attention to your starter and dough, and listen to what it needs. You will make mistakes and constantly question yourself. Every time something went wrong with my bread, I took it as an opportunity to learn and succeed. This book and the sourdough loaf records will help you do the same.

My sourdough story

My first memory of sourdough was aged nine. We'd been traveling to Dordogne for about 14 hours. As we approached the village that was to become the place we spent my remaining childhood vacations, I looked out of the car window: there was a fortress-like church with a huge bell, which was surrounded by fields full of fresh green grass, cowslips, and gnarled old walnut trees. We stopped at the hotel restaurant, and I got out of the car. I remember how happy I was as we were brought *potage,* and baskets filled with hunks of fresh-cut bread. It was so different from the bread in England. The crumb was chewy, and tasted lightly sour, and the crusts were as rugged as the bark of the walnut trees. At that moment I fell in love.

It turned out that the local bakery was just yards from our house, and so by the time I was 11, I was working there. I'd sweep up, knock out, and stack up the bannetons (wicker baskets), brush down the loaves as they came out of the oven, and serve the customers. I was often given some dough to shape, and allowed to bake it. Everyone from the village, rich and poor alike, bought their bread fresh every morning. I knew everyone, and everyone knew me.

I'd leave the bakery mid-morning and take the bread to the restaurant, where I would help Angelique in the kitchen, stirring the soup, fetching butter from the farm, pitting wild plums for tarts and feeding the carrot tops to the rabbits. As I got older, I would waitress, often serving the same people I'd served in the bakery earlier in the day. After lunch, I'd carry the previous day's bread in a sack back to my friend Noel's farm, and feed it to the pigs.

Back in the UK I left school, and trained as a chef and baker, then, at the age of 18, I returned to France, and promptly fell for a handsome Frenchman from the local village. His father got me a job as an apprentice in the local town bakery where I stayed for a year, baking sourdough, brioches, tarts, and patisserie. It was amazing, but the hours were long, and the pay minimal, and I wanted more, so I returned to the UK thinking I would put my skills to use in a British bakery. But in the early 1990s finding somewhere they baked sourdough was almost impossible. I was literally laughed out of one bakery when I explained how we fermented the dough using old dough from the previous day, otherwise known as *pâte fermentée* or pre-ferment.

Instead I found freedom working early shifts in a hotel making French patisseries. I was finished by 9 A.M., so during the day I went to university. I didn't sleep much at the end of my last term and I became ill. I was given large doses of antibiotics, after which, at the age of 24 and to my total dismay, I could no longer digest any wheat. The doctors couldn't explain why, so I stopped baking, changed careers, and followed a gluten-free diet for almost four years. It was miserable.

During this time I'd avoided France because bread was everywhere, but in 1998 I returned to show my now husband my French home. As I walked past the bakery on my first day back, I smelled the freshly-baked bread. Hervé the baker was so happy to see me, that he pressed a warm *miche (pain de campagne)* into my hands. It smelled so good. I found myself moments later at the kitchen table, oblivious to the rest of the world, devouring half the loaf in one sitting. My husband walked into the kitchen to find me sitting in a pile of crumbs, with my head in my hands, as it dawned on me that I was going to be ill... very ill. I braced myself for what was to come: asthma, joint pain, a foggy head, tiredness, irritability, bloating, eczema, and digestive issues. But, to my surprise, I wasn't ill. I was fine. I spent the next two weeks making up for lost time eating as much bread as I could. It was heaven. When I got home to the UK, I went out, bought a loaf of bread, ate it, and was promptly ill. It was then that I realized that the bread I had grown up eating in France was digestible, but the commercial bread I was eating in the UK was not. In that moment, the direction of my life changed, and I decided that I had to understand what was so different about sourdough.

As I began teaching, I figured that if I was to look after my students in the best way possible, I needed to know whether they had any health issues. I devised a form for the course bookings, which helped me to discover more about the health of my students. What soon became apparent, was that specific health issues kept cropping up—diabetes, IBS, Crohn's disease, diverticulitis, gluten sensitivity, and cancer. The students often had questions of their own; they came to me for more than just a formula. People wanted to understand sourdough, and to explore how it could contribute to their health and well-being. Increasingly, I realized that many people had the same questions I had. Why is sourdough easier to digest? As I began to talk about bread and digestibility, more people opened up about their digestive issues. There was never a class when someone didn't mention problems with digestion, and this raised more questions.

I started asking other bakers and healthcare professionals, but as no one was able to provide me with answers, I realized I was going to have to find the answers out for myself. I began to read every scientific paper I could find, and talked to microbiologists, gastrointestinal specialists, oncologists, and nutritionists. What quickly became apparent was that the fermentation is transformative, and the actions of the microbes have an extraordinary ability to change flour and water into something more nourishing and digestible.

The research also brought the role of other microbes to my attention. One research paper showed that some of the microbes in a starter originated from the soil when the wheat was grown organically. At the same time, I discovered that we have our own gut microbiome, and that having robust and diverse gut microbes is essential to our health. We are symbiotic with many of the same microbes. When you add in the process of fermenting bread, you complete a microbial circle from soil to our own digestion and health. The long, slow fermentation and acids produced by the lactic acid bacteria transforms flour to make a bread which is not just food for us, but provides sustenance to our microbe—sourdough is a prebiotic. It is astonishing. We are connected on levels that we are only just beginning to understand. In my determination to understand this incredible, transformative process, life has brought me full circle, and I am now chatting again to doctors about bread, only now it's about the School's nutrition and digestion of bread course—a course which has been accredited by the Royal College of General Practitioners.

So this book is far more than just a collection of formulas; it is about answering those questions, understanding sourdough, and sharing the knowledge of why this magical fermentation process is integral to making the most nourishing and delicious bread in the world.

How to use
this book

This book isn't about my bread. It is about your bread. I know my kitchen, I know my flour, and I understand the timings and process.

This book is about your bread, your kitchen, and your flour, and so to get the very best results, I have designed this according to my kitchen, and the flour that I use here. To succeed, you will need to plan. You can use my plan to begin with, but your flour and kitchen are different from mine, so follow my example, and then adjust timings and temperature accordingly.

1 Read the book before you start baking. Boring, I know, but you need an overall understanding.

2 Make sure you have all the equipment required (see page 200).

3 Start with the first formula (see page 114) and work your way forward. The formulas are in order of difficulty.

4 Go to page 70 and choose which method you want to use, either ambient (all in one day) or retarded (overnight in the fridge) according to your timings and taste preferences.

5 Go to page 73 and plan the schedule in conjunction with the formula.

6 Use the step-by-step chapter (see page 80) which gives detailed information on how to make your bread.

7 Record the timings and temperatures on your loaf schedule. You can photocopy this from page 73, or download more from sourdough.co.uk.

8 Analyze the results, and celebrate each loaf. Make notes on any adjustments you need to make. The more you bake, the better you will get.

Repeat.

Often.

Flour, water & salt + Culture, warmth & time = Sourdough

This is not just a recipe book; my aim is to challenge you to think about bread differently, because in spite of our ever-changing world, with its advances in modern technology, and the pressure to have everything done in an instant, bread is still the staff of life, something that every culture in the world has in common.

Sourdough is the oldest way of making bread, and uses naturally occurring wild yeast and lactic acid bacteria. It produces bread with a distinctive taste, but it is about far more than amazing flavor and nutrition. The process of baking sourdough is sensuous—it nurtures both mind and body, and requires a thoughtful and spiritual approach. Artistic and scientific, it is a combination of passion, patience, dedication, and craftsmanship. It is about connection, using hands, touch, smell, taste, sight, heat, and mind. These elements, which have been largely lost in the drive to make bread a commercially produced product, are not independent of each other; they are the cornerstones of sourdough. All of the formulas in this book are hand mixed, none are machine mixed.

The best bakers don't just blindly follow a formula. They use their senses. But before you can do this, you need to become familiar with the process, to the point where it becomes instinctive. You need to practice, in much the same way musicians practice their instrument, until playing it becomes second nature. Making sourdough takes more than just an ingredients list and a method. It means connecting with what you are doing, and getting to know the dough. The more you bake, the more familiar it will become. Good bakers bake often, and one of the best pieces of advice is to make more than you can eat: give your bread away. Find friends and neighbors to share your loaves with.

What is sourdough?

Sourdough is bread made from flour, water, and salt, and fermented using lactic acid bacteria and wild yeast. It is universal. The French call it *levain*, the Italians *lievito naturale*. The Russians say *zakvaska*, in Poland it's *zakwas*, Germans call it *sauerteig*, and in Denmark it's *surdej*. Spanish and Hispanic countries call it *masa madre*.

Sourdough is used as both a verb and a noun. It is a word used to describe a process of fermenting flour, water, and salt to make bread. The same word is used when talking about the bread.

Bakers culture and nurture a colony of symbiotic microbes in a pot of water and dough; this is called a starter. Some people love their starters so much, they name them like members of their family. Some go back generations, and are absolutely integral to daily life. Others are cultivated by home bakers, and occasionally emerge from the fridge, with the baker feeling guilty, like trying to revive an abandoned science project.

The key thing to understand, is that this culture is alive. Inside the pot is wild yeast and lactic acid bacteria. The lactic acid bacteria (LAB) produce organic acids that acidify the dough and transform the taste, nutritional value, and digestibility of the bread. It is predominantly the yeast that produces CO_2 that makes the bread light and airy, but it also makes other products that contribute to flavor.

The microbes in the pot work together, and the acid also provides protection to the acid-tolerant yeast cells from other competing microbes, so they can get busy producing enzymes, processing flour, and reproducing in peace. The enzymes are the key to breaking down the flour. There are lots of them, including amylase and maltase enzymes that break down the polysaccharides (a type of sugar), the complex starches in flour, and the maltose into simple sugars (glucose), making food available to all of the microbes, including the LAB. The yeast then produce another enzyme called invertase, which breaks down sucrose into glucose, fructose, and zymase. This in turn facilitates the fermentation of sugar into CO_2, raising the dough, and ethanol, which is involved in the formation of esters which flavor the bread. The lactic acids also contribute to kick-starting production of enzymes called physates, which break down phytic acid, making the bread more digestible and unlocking the nutrients, making it more nourishing. There is more on this in the digestibility and nutrition chapter (see page 182).

A starter needs to be replenished and maintained to insure that the activity of the microbes is managed. We refer to this as refreshing the starter.

For most people, the properties of wild yeast and LAB are an enigma; they just know that they flourish when maintained, and make great bread. However, as I explain later, different LAB produce different acids. These contribute to the variety of flavors and textures in sourdough. Some bacteria produce more acetic acid, others more lactic acid. The flavor and texture of your bread also depends on the kind of flour, the dough temperature, and length of fermentation.

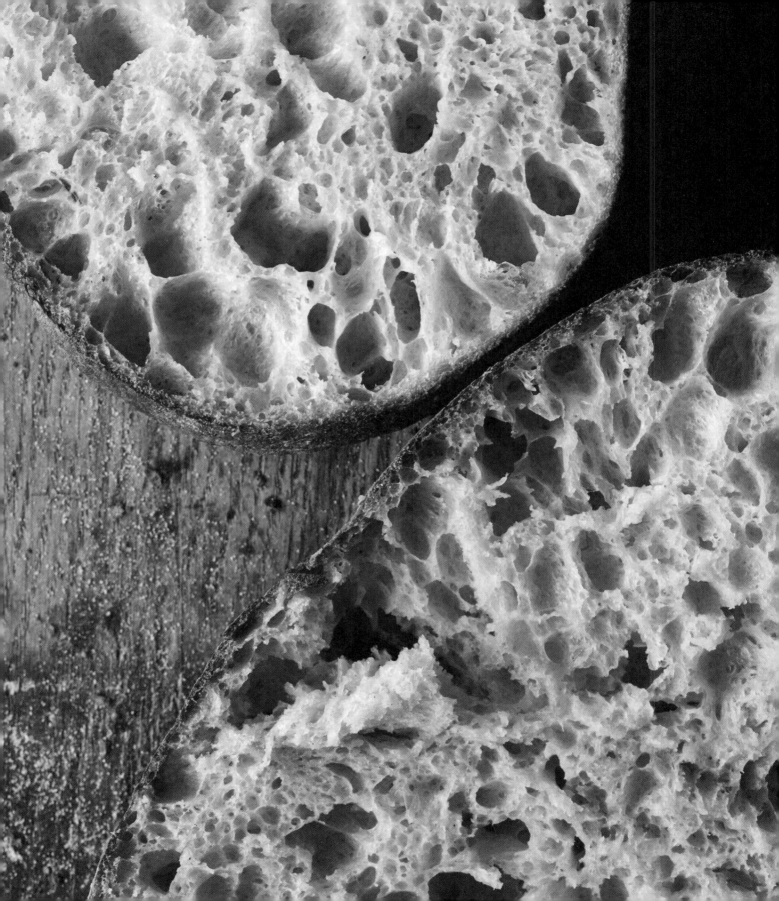

How sourdough works

There are some studies that indicate that the yeast and the bacteria have a mutually beneficial, interdependent relationship, sharing the available nutrients from the flour. Rather than compete for food, they act in partnership to protect their ecosystem from other uninvited bacteria. That said, it is actually more complex than this. There is generally one dominant yeast, and several lactic acid bacteria (*lactobacilli* or LAB). Perhaps a better way to understand sourdough is that bacteria are single-celled organisms, and lacking stomachs, they use enzymes to break down their food on the outside—in the dough.

I sometimes explain that sourdough starters are private members' clubs for microbes. As they produce acids as well as producing the unique flavors and textures of sourdough, the LAB are responsible for the increased acidity of the dough, which is one of the main reasons why sourdough is more nutritious and more digestible (see also page 186). They can be found in sourdough that has been slow-fermented at a bacteria-to-yeast ratio of 100:1. The yeasts—oval, one-celled fungi that produce carbon dioxide (CO_2) when they have access to oxygen through aerobic fermentation—are much bigger. They are the bubbles that you see in the bread dough, and are what makes your bread rise.

The job of the sourdough baker is to control the acidity variations of the dough through time, temperature, measurements, and the leavening, as the level of sourness affects the gluten structure, flavor, and crumb. So it is useful to

know where the acids come from and what they do. Understanding the microorganisms puts the baker in control of the baking process. The LAB break down the flour by the actions of enzymes, that in turn break down the starches into simple sugars. These sugars are then consumed by the microbes, which then produce both lactic and acetic acids that continue to break down the flour.

As the microbes produce acids, the pH of sourdough changes according to the stage of fermentation, but in general it has a pH of 3.5–5. It is this acidity that stops the development of pathogenic microorganisms such as *Clostridium botulinum*, *E. coli* and spoilage fungi, as they are unable to reproduce in an environment with a pH below 4.6. As well as producing these organic acids, the bacteria also produce exopolysaccharides, a kind of "sugar slime", in which they like to live. This slime has two main benefits: firstly it provides a structure and changes the "mouthfeel" of the bread, and secondly it provides food for our gut microbes.

The symbiotic relationship

Sourdough is a culture that relies on the relationship that exists between the lactic acid bacteria and wild yeast. In one of the earliest studies of the leavening action of sourdough by two researchers, Sugihara and Kline, conducted in the early 1970s, the principal yeast they found was *Candida milleri* (now known as *Candida humilis*) and the dominant lactic acid bacteria was *Lactobacillus sanfranciscensis* (a heterofermentative *Lactobacillus* species meaning that it produces more acetic acid). Unusually for yeast, *Candida milleri* likes to eat glucose and fructose, and is more tolerant of the predominantly acetic organic acids that *Lactobacillus sanfranciscensis* produces. *C. milleri* also doesn't digest maltose, which the *L. sanfranciscensis* loves.

This is a great example of how the microbe's choice of "food" affects the kind of bacteria that it hangs out with, and it explains why San Francisco sourdough is more sour. In simple terms, the *L. sanfranciscensis* has more "food" and so it produces more acetic acid, therefore the resulting bread is more sour. This is just one example of one starter—we are just beginning to understand these relationships, and we are learning that each sourdough starter culture has its own combination of individual microbes, and each colony is unique to its environment. There are many different combinations of bacteria and yeasts, all producing slightly different flavors, which become even more diverse when bakers start getting creative with their flour. Although there are sometimes several different kinds of yeast and bacteria in a starter, usually there is one dominant yeast and several more species of LAB.

What is clear is that the mix of microbes and yeast also depends on what the microbes break down, and what they then extract as food from the flour. Available "food", in other words, determines which microbes group together to form non-competing, symbiotic microbial clusters of species. Depending on the point in the process, some species compete with others for food. It is not quite so straightforward when there is both cooperation and competition at different stages of the fermentation process.

A sourdough starter is unique

At the Sourdough School I've seen and tasted starters from hundreds of bakers. Although they share characteristics, I am constantly astonished by the incredible diversity of flavors of both the starters and the sourdough breads. The idea that you can create an ecosystem in a pot that behaves differently according to the conditions in which it lives, and how it is nurtured is fascinating.

Research certainly seems to indicate that microbes in the pot are determined by environmental factors, including the flour, the soil in which the grain is grown, the environment in which it is kept, and wild yeasts in the air. I believe, however, that there is another influence in determining which microbes end up in starters. The cultures are nurtured by human hands, and I think that this interdependent relationship with the baker is the missing part of our understanding of where the microbes come from. In other words, the lactic acid bacteria in each baker's pot might well be influenced by the lactic acid bacteria from the baker's own skin microflora.

There were no studies on this as I began to write this book, but as I type these words, there is an amazing large-scale research project being carried out by Rob Dunn Laboratory looking into understanding more about cooperative microbial communities, and how their bacterial relationships work. So my theory that there is a possibility that starters are symbiotic with the baker and their skin microflora, will soon be better understood. During my investigations, I looked for more evidence of this relationship, so I had my own gut microbiome tested. There were absolutely no common microbes. I was somewhat disappointed, but as a friend pointed out, perhaps it was a good thing when you consider those might have ended up in the pot!

Ingredients

Baking sourdough is as much about connecting to your ingredients as it is to the bread itself. At the School, we try to use as much produce as possible from our organic garden, where we have an abundance of herbs, a walnut tree, and fruit, including blackberries, black currants, apples, pears, and apricots. The starting point for all ingredients, however, is the soil. My research into the subject has convinced me that we are part of a system that connects our well-being directly to the earth. It is a web—the soil is full of microbes, a sourdough starter is full of microbes, our digestive systems are full of microbes.

I'm often asked where the microbes in the starter come from. We know that the wild yeast and lactic acid bacteria hang out on the wheat itself, and one of microbiologist Marco Gobbetti's most interesting studies followed the life cycle from plant to flour. His team at the University of Bari looked at different farming practices, and the way in which soil is fertilized (or not), to see which method promoted the growth of bacteria on the wheat. The team grew durum wheat on the same farm using four different farming approaches:

▶ conventional
 (standard fertilizers and pesticides)
▶ organic with cow manure
▶ organic with green manure
▶ organic with no inputs

Even before the sourdough was fermented, there were differences in the composition of microbes in the flours. That derived from wheat grown in a conventional way had a higher amount of LAB from the genus *Leuconostoc* (19 %). After the sourdough fermentation, there were still differences. The flour derived from wheat grown using green manure, had the highest amount of *Lactobacillus*, and that from the flour grown using the no inputs treatment, had the greatest amount of *Leuconostoc*. The wild yeasts, however, were not affected by the farming method, and several species of yeast, including *Saccharomyces cerevisiae*, *Candida humilis/Kazachstania barnettii* and *Saccharomyces bayanus/Kazachstania* species or spp., were found in sourdough made using all four flours.

This study was the start of understanding that growing wheat by organic methods with the application of manure, is a source of microbes that make it into sourdough. In fact, there are more microbes in a teaspoon of soil than there are stars in the sky.

Why organic?

In 2013, Friends of the Earth Europe commissioned an independent laboratory in Germany to test people in 18 European countries for glyphosate, a herbicide routinely used on wheat. The results showed traces of glyphosate in an average of 44% of people, though in the UK 70% of people had traces of this weed killer in their urine. Dr. Robin Mesnage of the Department of Medical and Molecular Genetics at King's College, London, recently published a paper on the formulation of Roundup (the commercial name of glyphosate-based herbicides). He said: "Glyphosate is everywhere throughout our food chain—in our food and water. The lack of data on toxicity of glyphosate is not proof of safety, and these herbicides cannot be considered safe without proper testing. We know Roundup contains many other chemicals, which when mixed together are one thousand times more toxic than glyphosate on its own."

What I find particularly alarming is that worldwide usage of glyphosate has increased more than twentyfold since 1990, according to the Center for Biological Diversity, Tucson, Arizona. The conservation advocacy group says this upsurge is largely due to the widespread use of genetically engineered "herbicide tolerant" crops, particularly wheat and soya, which can withstand an otherwise fatal dose of glyphosate. In 2013, the Soil Association reported that nearly a third of UK cereals were sprayed with glyphosate, a total of almost 4 million square miles. Figures from government data analyzed by the Soil Association, which is calling for a UK-wide ban on the use of glyphosate, were released at a scientific briefing in London on 15 July 2015. These revealed that in the last twenty years, the use of glyphosate in UK farming has increased by 400%. Furthermore, it is one of the three pesticides regularly found in routine testing of British bread, appearing in up to 30% of samples tested by the Department for Environment, Food & Rural Affairs. The levels are well below the Maximum Residue Level (MRL) set by the EU, but a ban cannot come soon enough for me, because the truth is that no one can say with certainty whether glyphosate is safe, because long-term trials have simply not been done. The evidence has been drawn mainly from studies of agricultural exposures. Other evidence, including from animal studies, led the World Health Organization's International Agency for Research on Cancer (IARC) to classifying the pesticide as "probably carcinogenic" classification in March 2015. Research also indicates that chronic, low-dose exposure to glyphosate can cause liver and kidney damage, another serious concern apart from the decline in numbers of many pollinating insects that may be caused by spraying glyphosate.

The plant

Triticum aestivum, or bread wheat, is the most widely grown of all crops and represents about 95% of all wheat grown. A golden field of wheat with the wind sending rippling waves through it, is a beautiful sight to behold. We grow it in order to harvest the seeds, which are then ground into flour, though the grain itself grows with the intention of landing on the soil, getting damp and sprouting. The parent plant gives the seed everything it needs to do this: energy, which it stores as protein, and enzymes to break this down into easily accessible sugar; it is also packed with minerals and vitamins. Surrounded by a protective outer husk (the bran), this seed sits and waits for the perfect moment when water unlocks its potential.

When we harvest these grains and grind them into flour, the organic reactions remain the same, and as the enzymes break down the starch into sugar, so the lactic acid and wild yeasts benefit from the transformative abilities of the many enzymes. If you think about flour in this way, the whole sourdough process makes more sense. It reacts as though it is about to grow into a plant as you add the water.

Flour

To become a really good sourdough baker, you need to become familiar with your flour. All too often, bakers who lament their inability to create the bread they want, change their flour on an almost bake-by-bake basis. I often compare baking sourdough to playing a musical instrument. You can't start off learning to play all the instruments in the orchestra; you have to pick one, learn it, and then master it before you can do anything else. Likewise, the more familiar you become with one particular type of flour, the more you will understand its nuances. You'll see and feel how it begins to transform, and how it responds to different temperatures and different inclusions. Once you've become familiar with a particular type of flour, baking becomes much more instinctive. Then, when you move on to new flours, you'll find yourself able to bake with the understanding that comes from really knowing how the dough should feel, and you can adjust accordingly.

YOU NEED TO USE A STRONG WHITE BREAD FLOUR WITH 11–13% PROTEIN FOR THE BASE OF MOST OF THE FORMULAS IN THIS BOOK

The flour you choose will affect absolutely everything about your bread from the flavor down to the crust, crumb, texture, and rise. It always surprises me when I talk to bakers and they don't know where their flour comes from—and I don't just mean which mill or shop. I mean which field was the wheat grown in, which country, and how was it treated and by whom? A healthy plant will give you a better flour, so you need to know if it had access to nutrient-rich soil and whether the wheat was sown too closely together. Plants that were not sown too closely together will have a much deeper network of roots and will stand strong in the soil. It is via these deep roots that the wheat absorbs the nutrients it needs to grow.

Your flour—and therefore its level of gluten and how it behaves—is also affected by the variety of wheat the farmer has chosen to grow, and the *terroir*, or environmental conditions, in which it grows. Rather like roses in the garden, grain comes in many different varieties, all of which will have different perfumes, flavors, and textures. And, of course, sunshine is vital. In areas of higher sunshine, the wonderful warm rays produce a better quality protein. Protein itself is an energy storage unit for the plant, so the more energy it gets from the sun, the more storage units, i.e., higher levels of protein.

A guide to grains

BARLEY There are records of barley being used to make bread and beer in ancient Egypt, and Roman gladiators were known as "*hordearii*" or barley-eaters, in reference to the fact that their diets comprised large amounts of grain. Early farmers in the Fertile Crescent would have grown it alongside other ancient grains such as emmer and einkorn. It also grows well under cool conditions, making it well suited to more temperate areas and in countries where the climate is less favorable for wheat cultivation. It's high in fiber, low in gluten, and a good source of B vitamins, minerals, and protein. Barley has a variety of uses in breadmaking, either ground to make a flour, or added to the dough as a sprouted grain, or richly flavored malt extract. Barley is also a key ingredient in beer making and distilling. With a wide geographical spread, and thousands of years of domestication, there is now a range of barleys in cultivation. *Bere* is a six row variety of barley, cultivated in northern Scotland, and traditionally used to make bannocks. Two-row barley is used in beer making and black barley, originally from Ethiopia, is a tasty and highly nutritious ingredient.

BUCKWHEAT Another grain high in fiber, which therefore acts as a good prebiotic, has also been shown, especially when germinated, to produce lower GI responses. Its prebiotic properties have positive implications for obesity, and improving the gut microbiome. At the School, we use buckwheat as a porridge.

DURUM This is the only tetraploid [contains four sets of chromosomes] species of wheat of commercial importance that is widely cultivated today. Durum wheat flour is high in protein,

LONG, SLOW FERMENTATION IS A WONDERFUL WAY TO COAX THE MOST FLAVOR OUT OF GRAINS

however, it lacks strength, and so is often supplemented with refined wheat flour to offest its poor gluten network .

Interestingly, heritage durum wheat grains are often much more delicious than modern ones, and in some cases, they have higher levels of antioxidants. There is also evidence that the levels of healthy plant sterols (molecules associated with lowering cholesterol), are actually higher in tetraploid wheats like durum, than in hexaploid wheat varieties (modern bread wheat) so they are beneficial for heart health.

EINKORN This ancient wheat is a diploid variety, meaning it contains two complete sets of chromosomes, one from each parent. Like most heritage flours, it is incredibly flavorsome, being rich, nutty, and sweet. While it has low gluten levels, it is still a good source of protein, iron, dietary fiber, thiamine, and other B vitamins. It also contains a significant amount of the powerful antioxidant lutein, which makes it higher in antioxidants than durum and bread wheat. As it has remained unaltered for thousands of years, many people with gluten sensitivity report that they can eat it without an adverse reaction.

There is some evidence that einkorn has higher levels of phosphorus (phytic) compared to durum and hard red spring wheat, so although it is reported as being easier to digest, einkorn really needs a long, slow fermentation to neutralize the phytic acids for anyone suffering from IBS (see page 186).

EMMER A heritage Italian wheat (called farro in Italy) that has been around for more than two thousand years. The husk keeps the grain's nutrients intact long after it has been harvested, so every serving contains rich amounts of nutrients, including large amounts of fiber, vitamin B_3, and zinc. It is also a rich source of iron, with 110 grams containing 24% of the recommended daily intake.

FREEKEH A cereal grain made from green, young durum wheat that is roasted to create a nutty flavor. Freekeh is an excellent source of fiber and protein. It has double the amount of fiber of brown rice, and three times more protein than quinoa. It is also low on the glycemic index (GI), making it an ideal grain for diabetics.

KAMUT®/KHORASAN Kamut® is the commercial name for khorasan, an ancient wheat species with origins in central Asia. Golden in color, it is full of carotenes and selenium, and has a rich, buttery texture and complex flavor. It is a good alternative for people with type 2 diabetes, as research shows it helps to reduce glucose and insulin levels.

OATS Oats contain beta-glucans, powerful soluble fibers found in the oat's cell walls that reduce cholesterol in the body by preventing it being absorbed from the gut into the bloodstream. Beta-glucans also decrease the body's rate of starch digestion to keep blood sugar levels steady. One six-year study of more than 65,000 women found that dietary fiber actually prevented type 2 diabetes from developing. In fact, 4 grams of oat beta-glucans can lower glucose levels—by incorporating oats in their diet, some diabetics have seen a drastic improvement in their blood sugar levels. In another study in Norway, ten people were fed 60 grams of porridge a day, and found that within a week, their gut microflora had improved. At the School we use oats for porridge in the sourdough (see page 164), a suggestion for which I have to thank Richard Hart. I love adding porridge to bread, because it gives the most amazing texture, but the health benefits are also impressive.

RIVET WHEAT A heritage grain milled from a rare species of wheat (*Triticum turgidum*) which is absolutely delicious. It was first grown in England in the Norman period, and became popular because of its high yield and nutty flavor. Flour from these grains has less protein than others. Rivet flour (100%) could be a suitable alternative to whole-wheat for those with non-celiac gluten sensitivity, and is one I recommend trying as 20% in the classic formula, as it is a heritage grain.

RYE Has a distinctive, deep flavor. It is thought to have originated from a wild species that grew as a weed among wheat and barley fields. Sourdough breads made with rye are more compact and dense; its gluten is less elastic than wheat, so it holds less gas during the leavening process. Since it is difficult to separate the germ and bran from the endosperm, rye flour usually retains more nutrients, including higher amounts of fiber and phytonutrients than wheat.

SPELT This ancient grain is part of the same family as wheat, rye, and barley. Spelt is more easily digestible than wheat, because of lower levels of gluten, and higher levels of soluble fibers. Although the nutritional content of spelt is similar to wheat, it has almost double the amount of vitamin K (required for normal blood coagulation and optimum calcium absorption). It also contains several minerals including iron, potassium, and zinc, making it more nutritious than wheat.

WHEAT Wherever possible, I try to use whole-wheat grains. They contain both the bran and the germ, and are a high source of fiber, polyphenols, vitamins, and minerals (see pages 190–193). The long fermentation of sourdough increases the bioavailability of these beneficial components, making a more nutritious loaf compared to yeasted bread.

Gluten

Gluten is a protein that builds the network that keeps your dough together. It binds the starch almost like a web of rubber bands that runs through the bread, allowing the starch to gelatinize and stay in place. It works a bit like a balloon, capturing the carbon dioxide that comes off the microbes as they ferment the sugars in the flour, i.e., one with more protein content. You don't need very strong flour to bake great sourdough. Generally, I work with flour with about 11–13.5% protein. Occasionally I use a higher gluten flour to support lower gluten ones, and use it to blend.

Fermentation

The flour you use also dictates, to a large extent, the speed of fermentation. Flour contains amylase, an enzyme that breaks down carbohydrates into sugars that the yeasts can access. A flour's enzyme levels will depend on where in the world it was grown. British flours tend to have high levels of naturally occurring enzymes, because they are grown in a maritime environment. This results in high levels of enzyme activity, which means that dough ferments more quickly, yeasts are more active, and more carbon dioxide is produced, making the bread more bouncy and voluptuous. You will sometimes find flours that have had enzymes added to them—flours from the USA, for example, tend to have less naturally occurring enzymes, so millers make adjustments using malt and alpha-amylase to get the liveliness and activity needed.

STRETCHING AND FOLDING DURING THE BULK FERMENTATION HELPS DEVELOP THE GLUTEN NETWORK

Milling methods

The next thing to think about when choosing flour is the type of milling method used, because this makes a huge difference to your bread. When wheat is processed, the grain is crushed, milled, and then sifted to remove the germ and the fibrous outer layer. Traditionally, flour was stone-ground, but the modern milling process uses steel rollers. These rollers are very efficient at separating out the component parts of the grain, but they also get hot, which significantly reduces the number of wild yeasts and lactic acid bacteria that might be present in the flour.

All flours have an extraction weight, which is the percentage by weight that is extracted from the whole grain to make flour. You might assume that whole-wheat flour contains 100% of the grain, but this isn't always the case for highly processed flours. White flour still has very high levels of extraction—which can be up to about 70%—but what's left after the roller-milling process is pure endosperm or starch—the interior of the grain. As a result, white flour contains much lower levels of the micronutrients concentrated in the outer layers of the wheat germ (the aleurone). If you compare two white flours with a 70% extraction rate, one stone-ground and one roller-milled, the stone-ground one will still have some nutrients in it, but the roller-milled white one will have almost none. This means that some of the nutrients, such as calcium carbonate, thiamine (vitamin B_1) and iron, often have to be added in some countries, but not all. Not in France, for example.

The 40% of the grain that gets removed to make white flour includes the bran and the germ. These are the most nutrient-rich parts. In the process of making 60% extraction flour, more than half the vitamins and minerals are lost, including B_1, B_2, B_3, E, folic acid, calcium, phosphorus, zinc, copper, and iron, not to mention fiber. Despite this, organic roller-milled white flour can be an incredibly useful ingredient to blend with other flours, particularly if you want to add lightness to the texture of sourdough. I use strong white roller-milled flour almost as scaffolding, to add strength and to give a robust structure to my breads, and sometimes to slow things down, especially lower or non-gluten flours. However, I would never use 100% industrially milled flour on its own to make a loaf—not only is it lacking the key nutrients and fiber I want in my bread, but I find its flavor too flat, with none of the complexities of whole-wheat flour.

Milling your own flour

I love using freshly milled, whole-wheat flours in virtually every loaf that I make, so much so, that I have a collection of my own stone mills. When I use freshly ground flour, my breads have a subtlety and a richness of flavor that is an absolute knockout. There is a layer of wheatened "perfume" when you mill flour that elevates sourdough to another level of deliciousness. Commercial flour is all milled to the same specification. With your own mill, you can mill the same grain as coarsely or as finely as you want. This adds texture, and effectively adds another dimension to your bread.

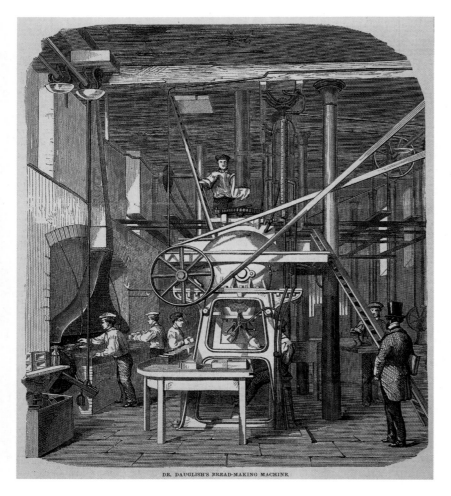

DR. DAUGLISH'S BREAD-MAKING MACHINE

I have several mills at the School. I love playing with the rough finishes that you can get using the hand mill—it is an ideal teaching tool because it's slow and considered. If you are in a hurry, a kitchen-top Komo mill has its advantages; flick a switch, and you are milling. The Mockmill is a lovely little attachment designed to fit a KitchenAid, and is a delight to use. If you already own a KitchenAid, then do consider getting a Mockmill—it's small, easy to use, and mills brilliantly. The main reasons for milling your own flour are flavor, flavor, and flavor. Stone-ground flour contributes significantly to increased flavor in slow-fermented breads. You get nuttiness,

malt flavor, and the sweet floral notes of dried meadow herbs, warming porridge, and toast to name just a few of the flavors found in whole-wheat sourdough. The higher levels of nutrients and the bran in whole-wheat accelerate fermentation and production of by-products, increasing acids and the metabolites, including iso alcohol, ethanol, ketones, and esters, and that brings wonderful complex flavors to the bread.

In terms of nutrition, there is no doubt that whole-wheat flour is more nutritious when fermented with sourdough. We explain more about this later in the book, as sourdough increases the bioavailability of the nutrients in bread. The outer bran layer of the wheat kernel (the endosperm) is incredibly rich in nutrients, and when you use freshly stone-ground flour, nothing has been oxidized yet, so it is as nutritious as it could possibly be. The germ contains lots of fiber, protein, vitamins, and minerals, which are vital for a healthy body and immune system. It is especially high in vitamin E, which is important for maintaining a healthy immune system, as well as healthy skin and eyes.

The other key component to stone-ground flour is that the body assimilates it more slowly than roller-milled flour. There is more fiber, which slows down the blood sugar response.

If you want to avoid all enzyme flour improvers or fortification then stoneground is a good choice. The FDA in America states that enriched flour must have minimum levels of vitamin B and calcium meaning it's often added, while other countries around the world have different flour enrichment programmes. If you are a purist and want to avoid these then the only way to do this is either by buying stoneground flour from small artisan mills, or by milling your own. Students often hear me saying that artisan bread begins with artisan ingredients.

Getting the best results from freshly-milled stone-ground flour

Freshly-milled flour is often referred to as "green". It is not actually green, it just has not had time to oxidize. Natural aging of the flour by exposure to the atmosphere, means that the flour has time to oxidize, which primarily affects sulphur-containing amino acids that are constituents of the gluten. The formation of gluten involves the creation of disulphide bonds, which hold the gluten together. Mixing also results in these bonds being formed, and the strengthening of the protein, which is what you need to make good bread. In short, you can make bread with fresh flour, but it is generally accepted that to in order to get optimal performance from your flour, it needs to age.

I have made bread with freshly-milled flour many times. It is possible to bake a beautiful loaf using freshly-milled flour, and I have not noticed a huge difference in volume. I don't have a technical explanation as to why you can successfully use very freshly-milled flour, but I suspect it is something to do with the oxygen levels in the flour being abundant as it is milled and the development of thiols. I also think that the higher enzymes and nutrients play a part in this. If anyone has a technical explanation then I'd love to hear more.

How to use stone-ground whole-wheat flour

Freshly-milled flour is surprisingly delicately flavored, but for maximum gluten development, aging it for a week or so will give you stronger gluten development. The first, second, and third formulas give a guide to using these. Be aware that some stone-ground flours can be trickier; initially they look like they can take more water, then slacken off after 20 minutes.

White versus whole-wheat

When blending flour, the next choice is whether you use a more high extraction flour or more whole-wheat. I've never much liked going from one extreme to the other—completely white roller-milled flour is missing some of the major component parts that make up the flavor and nutrition integral to sourdough bread. On the other hand, although 100% whole-wheat flour can be utterly delicious, enjoyable, and nutty, it can also, occasionally be heavy, leading to overly dense bread. More often than not, therefore, I find myself blending flours to get exactly the flavor and texture I'm after. You can blend either roller-milled or stone-ground white with whole-wheat flour.

Why we use artisan salt

Salt is vital for optimum health, and if we don't have enough, the body suffers accordingly. It is also essential for reasons of taste. Salt—and here I mean artisan salt—does more than improve flavor; it intensifies it. It reduces bitterness in food, enhances the sweetness, and provides balance. It aids in gluten development in breadmaking, and acts as a natural preservative, and, amazingly, it does all of this without adding any calories.

Salt making was, up until the industrial revolution, an artisanal craft. Much like breadmaking, salt too is an artisan product that has been industrialized, so we use a hand-harvested salt in our bread.

Table salt, sodium chloride, however, is a refined product, one that is devoid of minerals and is manufactured, in many cases, without any regard for the environment. So chemically manufactured table salt has no place at the Sourdough School. To those who think that artisan salt is simply for food snobs and wealthy people who can afford it, I say think again. Not only is it the most ethical and sustainable kind of salt to bake with, it is also the most nutritious. Sea salt is full of iodine, and in the various pink, red, and grey salts you can literally see the minerals. Plus almost a year's worth of sea salt to make bread weekly costs less than a pint of beer in my local pub!

AVOIDING SALT

You should never completely avoid using salt in sourdough—it has significant gluten-strengthening properties, provides the base for the flavors, and helps to control the speed of fermentation. If your doctor has advised you to cut down on salt, you can reduce the amount used by half, but to compensate, please add miso, soy, or a good rehydrated finely chopped seaweed, such as dulse. This will give you more minerals, and compensate for the lack of flavor, plus the extra minerals will go some way to help strengthen the dough. (As a guide I use about 5–7 grams of dry seaweed, which is then rehydrated to replace half the salt. See the miso & sesame bread on page 156).

Water

Sourdough bakers often overlook the importance of water. We can talk for hours about the nuances of the flour, but actually water is key to the success of the loaf too. How much to add, when to add it, and the temperature all contribute significantly to the finished loaf. The most important thing to remember, though, is that you should NOT add all the water at once when you mix.

One of the key processes of a beautiful open crumb sourdough is developing gluten when mixing, but if you add in all the water at once you will get a soup-like consistency. You have to hold back some of the water. As a rule of thumb, I mix almost all my white dough at 70% hydration (so 700 grams of water to 1 kilogram of flour). The remaining water is set aside, and added gradually once the gluten has been developed. This is a technique called *bassinage*. The exception to this rule is with whole-wheat, which requires more like 78–85% hydration. I apologize for being vague. This is the bit where you will need to use your judgement. It is why I recommend baking the classic loaf first, so you have a point of reference.

ADJUSTING THE INITIAL WATER
For some white flours, 70% hydration will not be enough, especially if you are working with a higher protein flour such as Khorasan, durum, or Canadian, or occasionally, a stone-ground white. The range for these flours is somewhere between 70–80%, although it can be up to 85%. Much will depend on the amount of fiber and protein in your flour, how it has been milled, and its age. The amount of water you initially use is also dependent on whether you choose to do a pure autolyze, or (as we do in most formulas) an autolyze with leaven. You will need very slightly more water if you follow a pure autolyze. So, despite wanting more than anything to give you an exact amount, you have to use your judgement.

THE REMAINING WATER
Almost all the remaining water is used for the *bassinage* technique (see page 98), but about 25 grams is used to mix the salt at the end of autolyze (it facilitates the salt distribution), and another 25 grams or so is used in the stretch and folding during bulk fermentation. The gluten carries on developing during bulk fermentation, and stretching and folding gives the dough structure, but you need to be gentle, so the very last of your water is used on your hands to stop the dough from sticking.

Here is an example of how you use a total of 850 grams of water:
700 grams in the initial mixing to autolyze (with or without leaven)
25 grams of water to incorporate the salt (at the end of autolyze)
100 grams added incrementally in 3 equal amounts during mixing (once the salt has been mixed in very well)
25 grams to use in the stretch and folds

The key to success is adding the water a little bit at a time, so that the flour has time to absorb it. If you get in a pickle, and your flour cannot take all the water, STOP. Relax. Walk away from the dough and make a cup of tea. Come back after a few minutes and assess it.

THE AMOUNT OF WATER
This is really important. I am not in your kitchen and I do not know your flour. The formulas have been developed using the ones I use. Some flours, especially those containing less protein, just need less water. If you find that there is too much water in the formula, then feel free to reduce it until you find the right

hydration for your flour—assess, record, and then try using more next time. Alternatively, if you find your flour super absorbent, or you feel comfortable adding more water, then do so. Slowly. You can always add more but you can't take it out! Just remember, the key is to add the water a little at a time between mixing.

WATER TEMPERATURE

The temperature of the water is a control. It acts like both the brake and the accelerator in a car. You can use warmer water to get to the desired dough temperature, or you can use colder water. When hand mixing I use water at about 86°F to allow for the fact that the temperature will drop as I mix. When machine mixing I use water at about 68°F as the friction of the machine will increase the temperature of the dough as it mixes. In summer you can reduce the temperature even further. Conversely, in winter, if your flour is cold, you may have to increase the water temperature to compensate.

TIPS FOR ADDING IN THE WATER IN THE AMBIENT VS. RETARDED

In the retarded method, the mixing in of the water is vigorous. In the ambient method, it is far gentler. I recommend dimpling in your fingers and adding the last of the water with the salt very gently and slowly, so as not to completely de-gas the dough.

THE MYTH

I also want to dispel a myth. You do not have to filter your water, or let it stand for hours. In highly chlorinated areas, you can leave your water on the side for 20 minutes before you use it. Do not use cool boiled water or mineral water. They are deoxygenated, so are not great for microbial activity.

Dried sourdough: using up leftover starter

There are several reasons for drying sourdough to a powder, not least the fact that it is a great way to use up the excess when refreshing your starter—no one wants to discard any. Dehydrated sourdough makes a superb flavor addition to the outside of a loaf, and I often use it to dust bannetons. When combined 50:50 with rice flour, it is especially useful for adding extra texture and flavor to the outside crust. You can also get creative with the flavors, and use them to enhance so many everyday dishes, from cakes and pastries, to mashed potatoes and muffins. I find it tempers sweetness, and the added acidity can balance flavors.

Some of the best flavored powders are made simply by sprinkling a tablespoon of a spice or herb into starter that is being discarded before smearing it thinly onto either a silicon mat or parchment paper. Then dehydrate for 3–7 days (somewhere warm and dry, such as a warm cupboard or a sunny windowsill). Remove the now dry flakes from the paper, and store until needed. You simply grind the flakes into powder using either a mortar and pestle, or a flour mill, and use as needed. These keep fresh for about 6 weeks in a sealed jar once dry.

BLACK CURRANT AND FENNEL

I like to use the white French starter (see page 62) for this, as, after 2 days, it has a slightly citric flavor. Smear the starter over the parchment paper and scatter with fresh black currants and a tablespoon of fennel seeds. Leave to dehydrate somewhere dry, such as a warm cupboard, for about a week. This works really well in a morning smoothie—a tablespoon per glass adds tang as well as supporting the gut microbiome as a probiotic.

CHARCOAL

Charcoal adds drama, but also tempers the acidity of the ferment, producing one of the sweetest ferments. I believe this is down to the fact that it is alkaline, and so reduces the acidity. To make a charcoal ferment, simply replace 20–30 grams flour in your starter with food-grade charcoal powder. Or you can make a ferment especially for powder with a tablespoon of starter, 20 grams charcoal powder, 40 grams white flour and 60 grams water. Ferment for a week in the fridge, then smear this over some parchment paper, and leave to dry (this one usually takes just 2–3 days). I love this as a dusting powder to enhance the color of the darker breads, such as the Russian Rye Bread (see page 127).

BEET AND BLACK PEPPER

Ferment 60 grams cooked beet purée with 40 grams white flour and 20 grams rye flour at room temperature for 48 hours to get a really sour tang. Spread over parchment paper and add a good ½ teaspoon of cracked black pepper. This is delicious added to a dukkah spice mix.

MINT

This is one of my favorites. Blend a small handful of fresh mint into 100 grams cold tap water. Mix this water with a tablespoon of starter and 120 grams white flour and ferment at room temperature for 8 hours before putting it in the fridge for 24 hours. Spread over some parchment paper, and leave to dry (usually 2–3 days). The cold water and cold fermentation encourage the acetic acids to develop, and you get a vinegary, minty tang from this powder. A tablespoon is great mixed into bread crumbs to make lamb burgers.

PARMESAN, GARLIC, AND ROSEMARY

This one is easy. I simply use the discard from a whole-wheat starter and scatter over about 2 tablespoons of grated Parmesan, then some freshly chopped rosemary, and 3 minced garlic cloves. It is best dried somewhere warm, such as a warm cupboard. I love this as a dusting on cheesy muffins, just before they go in the oven, or on top of fish pie.

PUMPKIN AND CINNAMON

Ferment 60 grams cooked pumpkin purée with 60 grams white flour at room temperature for 48 hours to get a really sour tang. Spread over parchment paper and add a good ½ teaspoon of ground cinnamon. This is really wonderful as a dusting on pumpkin pie, mixed with a little confectioners' sugar. It is also great mixed with a small amount of superfine sugar and sprinkled on top of a cappuccino, providing a gorgeous sweet–sour spicy tang.

CHOCOLATE

I usually use my chocolate starter (see page 85) to make this. I find that after a week it takes on almost balsamic vinegar sweetness. If you don't have a chocolate starter in the fridge, you can easily make chocolate ferment by mixing 20 grams raw cacao powder with 40 grams white flour and adding a tablespoon of starter, with 60–70 grams of 98.6°F water. Leave somewhere warm for 24 hours. Once fermented, spread over some parchment paper, and scatter with a tablespoon of cacao nibs. Leave to dehydrate somewhere warm and dry, such as a warm cupboard, for 4–5 days. This is excellent for dusting chocolate truffles with.

PAPRIKA

Smear about 120 grams of leftover sourdough over some parchment paper and dust with a generous tablespoon of paprika—this is absolutely delicious used in omelets, and as a finish to garlicky pan-fried cheesy potatoes.

SOURDOUGH POWDERS ARE AN INTERESTING WAY TO MAKE USE OF THE COMPLEX, SWEET AND SOUR FLAVORS CREATED BY YOUR STARTER IN OTHER EVERYDAY FORMULAS.

Sprouting

To understand sprouting, it helps to visualize what is happening inside a seed. Once you start the germinating process by providing warmth and moisture, the dormant seed starts to become a live plant. It changes both inside and out, so, when you eat that seed, you're no longer eating just a seed, you're eating a tiny plant.

Soaking helps reduce the fat content, which also helps convert the dense protein in the seed to simpler amino acids that are easier to digest. The enzymes are activated, and kick in to break down the complex carbohydrates into simpler glucose molecules.

Why sprout grains?

Sprouted grains are plump, and have an irresistible texture, sort of knobbly, and a sweet flavor. They add a moistness to bread that cannot be replicated by any other ingredient.

Sprouting grains also significantly increases their nutritional and bioactive content—especially the vitamin B content, particularly of B_2, B_5, and B_6—as well as improving palatability. In addition, germinated grains contain substantial amounts of total phenolics (see page 192), and rye has significantly higher content compared to non-germinated grains. These phenolics help reduce the risk of diabetic agents and cancers, including colon cancer.

If you have a particularly sensitive digestion, I recommend you sprout all your seeds, including sprouting and drying the ones you use to roll on the outside of your bread.

HOW TO SPROUT

You can sprout any grain, and there are several ways to use them, including:

▶ **directly in the bread—I add between 15 and 25% of the weight of the flour. Using more is fine, but the dough can get heavy. Either put in a blender and turn into a mash, or use whole.**

▶ **to make malt powder (see page 51).**

1 First rinse the grains, and then soak them overnight in a bowl of cold water, using double the weight of water to grains. The grains will roughly double in size.

2 After soaking, drain and rinse well, but don't touch the grains, as this can transfer unwelcome bacteria on to them—use a clean spoon instead. Put in a clear glass jar, cover with a piece of cheesecloth, and secure with string or a rubber band. Leave to stand at room temperature for 48–72 hours, away from direct sunlight. The grains need oxygen, so if they look too packed together, lift them using a clean fork to aerate. Rinse them once a day with fresh water.

3 When your shoots are slightly smaller than the grains, the sprouts are ready to use either directly into your bread, or to make malt (see page 51). Occasionally you will need to rinse and drain them before drying, as they will have developed a cheesy smell if they have been too closely packed together. Once dried, you can refrigerate them for a few days, but I find it is best to use them immediately.

Sprouting seeds

For many of the same reasons that we sprout grains, we also sprout seeds. Nuts also benefit from overnight soaking before use. These are some of my favorite seeds to sprout.

AMARANTH Although often referred to as a grain, this is the seed from a flowering plant. It is gluten-free and contains three times the average calcium of other grains. The bioactive peptides in amaranth (called lunasin) have been shown to have cancer-preventative benefits, and antihypertensive properties.

FLAX High in omega-3 fatty acids, these seeds are also a good source of protein and fiber.

SESAME Quite possibly my favorite seed. They are a great source of iron, vitamin B_1, zinc, selenium, and dietary fiber. In addition to these important nutrients, sesame seeds also contain two unique substances: sesamin and sesamolin. Both of these belong to a group of special beneficial fibers called lignans, which have been shown to have a cholesterol-lowering effect.

PUMPKIN These are packed full of nutrients, providing substantial quantities of healthy fats, magnesium, and zinc. Pumpkin seeds contain antioxidants such as carotenoids and vitamin E, which can reduce inflammation and protect your cells from harmful free radicals and many different diseases.

Malt

At the School, we add a tiny amount of malt powder when using white roller-milled flour as the main flour in the loaf (10 grams per kilogram of flour), but it is worth checking your flour as some already contain malt. The malt contributes to the goldenness of the crust, and the food available to the microbes boosts your sourdough, giving a good rise and golden color.

Malting grain is the slow, gentle process of sprouting, drying (or roasting), then milling grain. Apart from the color and flavor this process adds, malting is used by brewers, whiskey distillers, and bakers to harness the ability of naturally occurring enzymes to convert starches into simple sugars. There are two types of malt, based on the presence or lack of enzymes they contain:

DIASTATIC MALT has enzymes that are still active. The enzyme's job is to convert starch into sugar, so by adding diastatic malt to dough, you are further increasing the sugars made available to the microbes.

NON-DIASTATIC MALT, which has been heated to a higher temperature to bring out flavors, stops the enzymatic reaction.

You don't have to make your own malt. You can buy it easily from a good supplier of baking ingredients and equipment—or find a local brewer. They will have dozens of different flavors, including malted oats and chocolate malt. We generally use local barley to make the malt we use at the School.

A step-by-step guide to homemade malt

Malt deteriorates over time, so I tend to make it three or four times a year to keep it fresh. Store in a clean, airtight jar for up to six months. You can make malt from various grains, including wheat, spelt, rye, and barley. The process takes 6–7 days.

1 First sprout 200 grams of grains (see page 48) (you tend to get just a bit less than the amount you started with, so 200 grams of grain gives you about 175 grams of malt).
2 Next you need to dry or roast the grains.

EITHER Drying can take up to 24 hours or even longer, depending on the size of the grain. I leave mine in the oven at just below 104°F (any hotter than this and the enzymes will not survive) until they are completely dry—taste one to check; if it is hard and crunchy it is dry. Mill these to set diastatic malt.

OR Roasting the sprouted grains intensifies the flavors. As the starches and proteins brown (the Maillard reaction), various flavor and color compounds are produced. This kills the enzymes (so it's just flavored food). See below for temperatures and timings.

OVEN TEMP	DRY/WET	TIME	FLAVOR
285°F	Dry	1 hour	Light nutty
350°F	Dry	15 minutes	Light nutty
350°F	Dry	30 minutes	Toasty nutty
350°F	Wet	1 hour	Light, sweet, toasty
350°F	Wet	1½ hours	Toasted malty, slightly sweet
350°F	Wet	2 hours	Strong roast

3 Mill or grind the grains into a flour using a mill, or mortar and pestle.

4 Transfer to an airtight jar and store in the fridge. Malt is better slightly aged, and the more you roast the grains the longer you need to age them—sometimes I leave the very dark ones for up to two months before using.

Smoking

Adding a layer of smokiness to your bread can create a whole new dimension, and it is one of my favorite ways to play with flavor. It's like a painter being given an entire new palette. Think spelt smoked with applewood, beechwood-smoked rolled oats, or smoked kibbled rye combined with dried wild cherries (see page 154). A word of caution though: a light touch is far more suggestive and delicious, so aim for subtlety.

You can include a smoky note in a number of ways and to different degrees: by smoking grains and then milling them into flour; by smoking grains after they have been sprouted (be sure not to get them hot—they will need to be cold-smoked) and then using them directly in the dough; or smoking the whole loaf once it has been baked.

Generally, most woods are fine to smoke with (see list on facing page), but some are poisonous (yew and laburnum) and some will have been treated with chemicals that are poisonous. Others just taste revolting. Never use wood from conifers such as pine, fir, cyprus, spruce, redwood, or cedar—they contain too much sap and also taste horrible. Freshly cut "green" woods will also have more sap, and can produce bitter notes. Never use wood that has been painted. Most of the wood I use for cold smoking comes from the gardens at the School, and the best time for collecting it is winter or very early spring, before the sap rises. I prefer air-dried wood chippings, as the wood is slightly wetter than kiln-dried—the water provides steam that makes the droplets larger and stickier, and you get a better, rounder smoky flavor. Or you can simply buy ready-prepared, food-grade wood chippings.

The subject of smoking food is so vast that it merits a book in its own right, but there are basically two techniques for sourdough: the first involves smoking the ingredients, the second the finished loaf. Smoking the ingredients results in a subtler flavor throughout the loaf, whereas smoking the entire loaf results in a more intense smokiness, with the aroma predominantly concentrated in the crust.

I hot-smoke in a cast-iron Dutch oven using an upturned foil takeout container, as in the photograph here, though if you prefer, you can buy a ready-made one. I place the wood chips in the bottom of the pot, then cover them with the foil container, having first punched a few holes in the top with a sharp pencil. I then place the grains or loaf on top, put the lid on, and place over a high flame on the stove for 2–3 minutes until I see smoke seeping out from the sides. I then turn it off and leave it until it is cold.

AN OLD POT WITH A LID AND AN UPSIDE DOWN FOIL TAKEOUT CONTAINER MAKE EXCELLENT HOMEMADE SMOKERS

Woodsmoke flavors

APPLE Mild with a fruity flavor, slightly sweet

ASH Light, but distinctive flavor

BIRCH Not dissimilar to maple

CHERRY Mild aromatic and fruity. Wonderful flavor

CRAB APPLE Similar to applewood

GRAPEVINES Very smoky rich and fruity

MAPLE Smoky, mellow, and slightly sweet

OAK My favorite. Very classic, and very French

PECAN Sweet and mild with a flavor similar to hickory

SWEET FRUITWOODS (APRICOT, PLUM, MULBERRY) Mild and sweet

WALNUT Very heavy smoke flavor, usually too strong for my liking

The foundation of your loaf

The basics: the starter

Before you begin, you need a starter, and to understand how to create and look after it. You can make your own by capturing the wild yeasts and bacteria already present on the grains that your flour is milled from. This is fun, and will give you a huge sense of satisfaction, but it takes a little time. Depending on the ambient temperature of your room, and the microbial activity of the flour you are using, it can take from three days to two weeks, so if you are full of enthusiasm about starting baking, I suggest that you begin by making a loaf with a thriving starter that is already producing great loaves for someone else. If you don't have a baking friend who will give you a small amount of their starter, you can buy an established one from one of the online resources (see page 202). Scientific studies indicate that an established starter is stable, active, and resilient, and in your first attempts at making sourdough bread, it will guarantee a better loaf, which is more likely to keep you baking.

WHAT IS A STARTER?

Sourdough is a symbiotic microbial ecosystem made up of wild yeasts and lactic acid bacteria that have colonized the mixture of flour and water. The behavior and the characteristics of your starter depend on the type of yeast and lactic acid bacteria, which in turn depend on the temperature at which your starter is refreshed, the kind of flour used to maintain it, and the resident bacteria in the environment that it is kept in.

DO I NEED TO UNDERSTAND THE MICROBES TO MAKE GREAT SOURDOUGH?

No—people made bread for thousands of years before we even invented microscopes or knew of their existence—though a basic knowledge will help you better understand how to change the flavor of your bread. At the School, we have students from all over the world who want to understand how they can use fermentation to experiment with flavor, and make more nutritious bread. Controlling the levels of acid in the dough influences the flavor and the level of sourness, which in turn affects the gluten structure, texture, and crumb of the bread. So it is very useful to understand where the acids come from, and what they do.

WHERE DO THE BACTERIA COME FROM?

The flour that you use to refresh your starter is a major influence on the kind of bacteria that colonize your starter.

WHAT OTHER FACTORS AFFECT THE STARTER?

The soil that your flour is grown in can affect the kind of microbes you get colonizing your starter, as can the environment in which you keep your starter, and the temperature at which you refresh it. The farming practices used to grow the grain (usually wheat) also affect the microbial composition (see page 26).

WHAT IS IN THE STARTER?

There are two kinds of microorganisms that cause sourdough to ferment: yeasts and lactic acid bacteria (LAB). These have a mutually beneficial symbiotic relationship, sharing the available nutrients from the flour. Mostly, rather than compete for food, they cooperatively protect their ecosystem from other uninvited bacteria.

There are about 23 known species of yeast, but the most common ones are *Saccharomyces cerevisae* and *Kazachstania*. The yeasts are tiny, oval-shaped one-celled fungi, though are much bigger than the LAB. When they have access to oxygen, aerobic fermentation produces carbon dioxide gas, which makes your bread rise.

Sourdough bacteria are predominantly *lactobacilli* and are also found in other fermented foods, such as kefir and sauerkraut. These bacteria are responsible for producing the unique by-products that enhance the flavors and textures of sourdough, in particular, producing the organic acids that change the pH of the dough.

HOW DOES SOURDOUGH FERMENT?

When the yeasts have access to oxygen, aerobic fermentation causes them to grow more cells. Once the oxygen is then used up, they change to anaerobic fermentation, which is much like fermenting beer; the yeasts make both alcohol and carbon dioxide gas (CO_2) using up the simple sugars that the enzymes have broken down. The bubbles that you see in the bread dough are the released gas, and are what make your bread rise.

At that same time the LAB which are responsible for producing the unique flavors and textures of sourdough, produce organic acids that change the pH of the dough, which is key to the increased nutritional value and digestibility of sourdough (see pages 184–193).

ARE THERE DIFFERENT KINDS OF LACTIC ACID BACTERIA?

Yes. There are many species that produce different flavors and textures, but LAB are categorized based on their by-products. The following terms might sound technical, but once you know that homofermentative LAB is the bacteria found in yogurt, it becomes more understandable.

SOUR, VINEGARY FLAVORS

Obligate Heterofermentative—Ferments glucose and produces ethanol and both acetic acid and lactic acid, as well as carbon dioxide (CO_2) as by-products, which produces a more sour and vinegar-flavored bread.

Facultative Heterofermentative—Produces mainly lactic acid, but in some cases, it can also produce acetic and lactic acids.

MILKIER FLAVORS

Obligate Homofermentative—Ferments glucose and only produces lactic acid as the primary by-product, which is milky, and produces a sweeter, more yogurt-flavored sourdough.

HOW DO THE BACTERIA AFFECT THE BREAD?

The bacteria produce organic acids that acidify the dough. This acidity is one of the main reasons sourdough is more nutritious and more digestible. Their other job is to produce exopolysaccharides, a kind of sugar slime that the bacteria like to live in. These exopolysaccharides have two main benefits. Firstly, they provide a structure and change to the mouthfeel of the bread—there are some specific bacteria, leuconostoc, for example, which have been identified for producing dextran, resulting in the voluptuous, soft, sweet mouthfeel of classic panettone. Secondly, exopolysaccharides make great food for our gut microbes, even when baked.

WHAT IS A TYPICAL SOURDOUGH RATIO?

In January 2017, the School's French white sourdough starter, derived from the original French starter from the bakery I grew up baking in, was analyzed by the Puratos Sourdough Library in Belgium. This analysis revealed that it contained one dominant yeast and several kinds of LAB, which is typical of the makeup of all starters.

We have four starters at the school, each one producing sourdough with different flavor profiles:

White – Sweet yogurt-like flavors
Yeast = *Saccharomyces Cerevisiae*
Lactobacillus kimchii
Lactobacillus sanfrenciscensis
Lactobacillus acidifarinae

Chocolate – Lactic, both tangy, milky, and fruity
Lactobacillus plantarum (43%)
Lactobacillus sanfranciscensis (38%)
L. fermentum (16%)
Fructoe pseudoficulneus (12%)
Acetobacter pasteurianus (8%)

Rye – Sour and deeper, darker treacle and complex flavors
Lactobacillus sanfranciscensis (32%)
Lb. acidophilus (22%)
Lb. pentosus (17%)
Lb. pontis (8%)

Whole-wheat – Sour and sweet malt and beer flavors
Lactobacillus acidifarinae (48%)
Lactobacillus kimchii (37%)
Lactobacillus sanfranciscensis (21%)
Lb. pentosus (13%)
Lactobacilli brevis (10%)

How to make a starter

To create your own sourdough starter I recommend using just two ingredients—organic stone-ground flour and water. It is important that the flour is stone-ground as some modern roller-milling heats the flour to temperatures that can reduce the naturally-occurring wild yeast.

Choose a warm room—not hot, not cold, just somewhere that is pleasant to be in. As the starter is acidic, and will react with certain metals, it needs to be made in a nonreactive container. I prefer glass, but plastic is fine too. You'll also need a whisk, to incorporate air, and a breathable cover, such as a clean dish towel, coffee filter paper, or a loose-fitting, disposable shower cap.

Begin by putting 150 grams organic stone-ground whole-wheat flour and 150g water heated to a temperature of 82°F in a large jar. Whisk the mixture vigorously and cover. Leave to sit in a warm place for 12–24 hours, but make sure there are no other cultured foods nearby ,or there will be a crossover, and you may not get the microbes you need. After this time, you might be lucky enough to see some bubbles, indicating that organisms are present, but if not, don't worry. Discard half the mixture and replace it with 75 gra,s flour and 75 grams water heated to 82°F. Stir vigorously, cover, and wait an additional 12–24 hours.

From now on, you will need to remove and discard half the starter before every feeding, so that the organisms in the starter can multiply without the jar overflowing. If you are somewhere warm, you will find activity begins quickly, usually after 3–4 days, but if you are in a more temperate climate, then it can take 10–14 days for the starter to become beautifully bubbly and have enough yeasts and bacteria to bake with. When you are developing the starter, keep it in a warm place to ferment. Once the fermentation is established, transfer the starter to the fridge.

You can start refreshing your starter according to the kind of bread you want (see pages 83–87).

WHAT BACTERIA CAN I EXPECT IN MY STARTER USING THIS METHOD?

You can expect to find a range of bacteria, but it's impossible to really tell without a laboratory analysis, though the bacteria will, of course, be different. Because the temperature at which the starter is kept is below 93°F, heterofermentative LAB (see page 61) will come to the forefront.

WHAT IF I WANT TO CHANGE MY STARTER TO A HOMOFERMENTATIVE LAB-DOMINANT STARTER?

If you want to change the makeup of your starter, take 25 grams of your original, and swap to the appropriate refreshment method. Generally this takes about 3–5 refreshments.

WHAT IF I WANT TO CHANGE BACK AGAIN?

This can be done, though I don't recommend frequently changing starter microbes. Starters seem most robust and reliable when refreshed consistently. In my experience, it takes longer to bring a sweeter, homofermentative starter back to being a predominantly sour heterofermentative than doing it the other way around. Perhaps 4–7 refreshments. Use cooler water for refreshing and always use whole-wheat or rye flour.

WHAT IF I WANT TO CHANGE MY STARTER PROFILE?

It is not as simple as changing the microbes. They will remain the same unless you change your refreshment schedule, flour, or environment. However, by changing the water temperature, you can encourage certain bacteria to come forward as a higher ration, which then affects the acids, and therefore the flavor. See page 83 for how to refresh your starter to achieve this.

WHAT IF IT STARTS TO SMELL OR LOOK HORRID?

Your starter should not smell unpleasant. Nor should it have black bits in it, or any mold. On rare occasions you may create a new starter only to find that it smells horrid, or that the bread and other baked goods it produces aren't very pleasant. If that's the case, it means that the bacteria that have populated your starter are not the right kind, and the lactic acid production, which makes the starter inhospitable to other organisms, hasn't got going. You will need to discard this starter and begin again, moving the location of your starter to a different room.

Usually, people who are having difficulties making a starter have meddled with the process. Please just be patient. Do not use hot water, it should be just warm (about 82°F) and there is no need to add any baker's yeast. You can add something likely to have wild yeast living on it, such as organic grapes, but, to be honest, the yeasts that you want to encourage are most likely to be found where they will get a decent meal, i.e., on the outside of the grains that the flour is milled from.

HOW DO I KNOW IT IS READY TO BAKE WITH?

See page 88.

WHAT IF I WANT TO GO ON VACATION?

I often leave my starter for up to two weeks without any ill effects. Some people like to leave it with a friend or neighbor, but if that is not an option, maintaining your starter becomes about leaving the microbes in a super-fit condition, and reducing the acidity. Before you go away, refresh your starter twice a day for two days, and in the final refreshment, thicken it, using about 60 grams water to 100 grams flour. Reducing the amount of water slows down the enzymes, which in turn slows down the rate of acidification. When you get back, build your starter back up again by giving it a good feed twice a day for two days. Then return to normal refreshment.

HOW LONG IS THE LONGEST YOU CAN LEAVE A STARTER FOR?

I've often joked that I run the RSPCSS—the Royal Society for Prevention of Cruelty to Sourdough Starters—not least because I have successfully revived a starter that has been neglected for over six months. It goes very smelly from the butyric and hexanoic acids—like Parmesan or old sneakers—and gets a dark "hooch" (see below) on top. Can you revive it? Yes, but it has to be built up again in the same way as starting from scratch. Is it worth reviving? Well, that depends on how attached you are to it. If the starter has a sentimental value, then perhaps it is worth doing. It will take a few days to get it going again with repeated refreshments, and sometimes it is simply easier to start again.

WHAT IF MY STARTER HAS A LAYER OF GRAY WATER ON TOP OF IT?

This is called "hooch." It is a protective layer of water and alcohol, keeping out unwelcome microorganisms. It simply shows that your starter has been left for a while and needs refreshing. Just follow the same procedure as the post-vacation refreshment (see left) to build it back up again.

WHAT KIND OF FLOUR SHOULD I USE?

The kind of flour you use is up to you. I've kept British white, rye, spelt, whole-wheat, heritage grain, and chocolate (using 20% cocoa powder) starters. I recommend three things, though. Firstly, that the flour you use is organic; secondly, that it is freshly-milled; and thirdly, that it is stone-ground. This will give your microbes the most nutritional support and reinforce their numbers, which supports the health of the ferment.

CAN I CHANGE THE FLOUR I USE?

Yes, although I favor continuity. But I have often needed to change flour for various reasons, and, over a couple of refreshments, the starter takes to its new food.

WHY DON'T MATURE STARTERS MAKE GREAT SOURDOUGH?

When the yeasts are in aerobic conditions, they are at their most active. When yeast ferments in the absence of oxygen (anaerobic fermentation) it produces alcohol and slows down, which is why a sourdough culture that has been left to ferment for a while without being aerated or refreshed, will develop a thin layer of water and alcohol (hooch) on the surface.

This alcohol provides a catalyst for additional flavor dimensions in the form of iso-alcohols, which contribute to the esterification of organic acids with alcohols. In other words, you get esters forming, which make your starter smell lovely—of fruit, such as ripe apples, pears, or pineapple. The reality, however, is that it is way too acidic. It needs refreshing (it is fantastic to use for a rye loaf!), but never more so than when the smell changes from fruit to nail polish remover (acetone) or even further down the line to old cheese (butyric acid). The truth is that while the esters in a mature starter smell delicious, they can't really be used because the starter is just too acidic at this point.

HOW MANY STARTERS DO I NEED?

One. Or perhaps two. I recommend keeping one hetero- and one homofermentative as this means you can bake both a sour, and sweeter milkier bread. But for beginners, the whole-wheat one is the easier and most versatile.

WHICH KIND OF STARTER DO YOU RECOMMEND?

That really does depend on your tastes and requirements. The most versatile starter is the whole-wheat as it can be easily converted into white, rye, or chocolate in just three or four refreshments over a few days.

HOW MANY STARTERS DO YOU KEEP AT THE SCHOOL?

I might give you a raised eyebrow look when you ask this. I have 5 or sometimes 6 or 7 or more … I have guest starters, some of which have stayed, most of which I abandon.

HOW DO I MAINTAIN MY STARTER?

See page 62. The way in which you maintain your starter can affect the kind of bacteria that flourish in it. I'm not suggesting that you can choose individual species, but rather that my suggestions are based on knowledge and understanding of which conditions various bacteria and yeast prefer. In other words, how you can encourage the kind of microbes that will give you the kind of results you want.

WHY WOULD YOU CHOOSE TO CONTROL THE KIND OF BACTERIA IN YOUR STARTER?

Ultimately it is about controlling the flavor and acidity levels of your sourdough. Some people want to enjoy naturally leavened bread that is not sour, while others love a really distinct tang. If you couple controlling the foundation of your loaf, along with the kind of fermentation method that suits your preferred flavored bread, then you can make the kind of loaf you really enjoy eating, or if you have issues with wheat intolerances, can digest.

HOW DO YOU CONTROL THE RATIOS OF BACTERIA THAT FLOURISH IN YOUR STARTER?

There are four suggested methods on pages 84–87 that explain how to do this. I cannot guarantee that these methods will give you the same microbes (there are hundreds of species), but rather this is a rough guide to how you can achieve similar results to the starters I have listed. There are many options to maintain starters, but my suggestions are based on the refreshment routines that we use at the School. The key to the kind of microbes that dominate your starters is the temperature. A temperature above 93°F encourages homofermentative bacteria to flourish. Below this, often the heterofermentative LAB bacteria come to the forefront.

The leaven

The leaven is often a point of confusion for bakers. Not all bakers use one, and it is called by many different names. In the same way that the Bible calls the devil by many different names, bakers have many names for their ferments. Each one has a slightly different meaning.

Some bakers refer to the leaven as a pre-ferment; even more confusing are the borrowed terms from other types of bread baking, such as *poolish* or *biga*. Leaven or, in French, *levain*, is also referred to as the "chief", "chef", "head", "mother" or "sponge." Other bakers simply use the word starter—which is even more misleading for home bakers. After all, your starter is a starter all the time. Even six months old, and smelling of cheese it is still a starter.

SO WHAT IS LEAVEN?

Leaven is the second build of your sourdough army of microbes—flour and water mixed with a small amount of your starter culture and fermented, to create an active colony of wild yeasts and *lactobacilli*. It is almost an exact repeat of refreshing your starter. It is mixed with the flour and water from the formulas, as the inoculation that ferments the dough.

WHEN SHOULD I MAKE A LEAVEN?

The ambient method leaven is made 8–10 hours before you mix the dough to make the bread. Generally, it is made with white bread flour (which ferments at a slower rate than rye or whole-wheat). Ideally, it is made late in the evening, just before you go to bed. The advantage of doing it then is that the leaven is ready to be used when you wake up, the bread can be put in the oven in the late afternoon, and you have a freshly baked, perfectly cooled loaf to enjoy in the evening. I don't recommend leaving the leaven much longer than 8–10 hours, as it will become too acidic. It's not the end of the world, but the volume of the loaf will be compromised over a long, slow ferment.

The retarded method leaven uses whole-wheat or rye flour to make the leaven, which ferments faster. As the dough for this method ferments for longer, it is best to use a young leaven, one that is about 2–4 hours old. The timing for this means that you make the leaven about 8 A.M. and it is ready to use at midday. I don't recommend leaving it longer than 4 hours. The more you bake, the more familiar you will become with the rhythm of the bake.

WHY IS IT IMPORTANT TO USE THE LEAVEN WHILE IT IS FRESH?

It is especially important to use a leaven while it is still young and fresh, because too much acidity will not only overpower the delicate flavors of the flour, but will also degrade the gluten in the dough, which means you lose volume. I tend to think of leaven as being young, fresh, and sweet. The sour flavors develop as the dough ferments. Even if you want a sour flavor, you still use a young starter.

DO I STILL USE A YOUNG, FRESH LEAVEN IF I LIKE SOUR-FLAVORED BREAD?

You still use a young, fresh leaven. You refresh your starter to develop the kind of bacteria that gives you the flavor you like, and retard the dough to give the LAB time to create acids as the dough proofs. By doing it this way, you are able to build a strong gluten network, as the dough is mixed in an acid-free dough that facilitates strong gluten development, and so you get both a well-sprung loaf, and a sour tangy flavor through the long, slow cold proof.

SO WHY MAKE A LEAVEN IF A BAKERY SIMPLY USES A STARTER?

A bakery makes bread every day. Home bakers generally bake once a week; enthusiastic ones twice. If you've become slightly obsessive, maybe four times a week. As your starter ages, it acidifies, and refreshing it every 8 hours is not practical—trust me, I have tried it and it is an exhausting routine. By making a leaven, you can refresh less often, and still get a loaf with a great spring by building up the levels of microbes. To borrow the words of Richard Hart, "Sourdough bakers are yeast farmers. Our job as bakers is to multiply yeast numbers." It's a bit like getting the most workers possible to build a pyramid: the more you have, the easier it is to get the job done. The yeast's job is to create carbon dioxide; so making a leaven using a recently refreshed starter is the easiest way to ramp up the numbers of yeast. This way they are young, vigorous, and enthusiastic. It is also, as importantly, a means of controlling the acidity.

HOW DO I INSURE A VIGOROUS LEAVEN?

Always refresh your starter the day before you make your leaven (see refreshment guidelines on page 83). This will insure you achieve a really vigorous leaven, as you will be building your leaven with a starter that is biologically at its microbial peak.

HOW DO I KNOW IF MY LEAVEN IS RIPE AND READY TO GO?

The most common test—providing your starter is made using predominantly white flour—is to see if a small teaspoon dropped in a glass of lukewarm water will float. However, this alone does not indicate it is at perfect ripeness. The second thing to do is to smell and taste it. Please don't pull a "not likely" face—baking is something that involves all your senses and you need to be intimate with your culture. You only need about ¼ teaspoon. It should smell lactic, wheaten, yogurty,

and still a little bit floury, and taste lightly yeasty and sweet. You should then get a slight tang, which will be almost undetectable.

The leaven will also float when it is too acidic and has gone too far, which is why you should do the taste test. You'll be able to taste the acidity, which has a citric quality similar to that of lemons, light and very tart. If you are fermenting your dough for long periods in the fridge, the bacteria have a chance to produce even more acid, resulting in a flatter, sourer loaf.

CAN I CONTROL THE TIMINGS OF WHEN A LEAVEN IS USED?

You can slow the speed at which the leaven matures by reducing the amount of water to 60 grams per 100 grams of flour (60% hydration), which keeps it sweeter for longer, in effect buying you an additional 2 hours or so in which to use it. This is useful if you are working shifts, are a professional baker with several batches to mix, or if you just want to stay in bed longer. You can also drop the water temperature to 64–68°F. It is best to use one method at a time, however, and to get used to the fermentation rates for that one, rather than changing methods. The rate of fermentation is also subject to ambient temperature changes. It is difficult to be precise about these, but as a rule of thumb, the warmer the ambient temperature, the faster the leaven will ferment.

You can increase the speed at which the leaven matures by using whole-wheat or rye flour to make it, and by increasing the water temperature to 86°F and maintaining this temperature during fermentation. This will mean your leaven will be ready in 1–2 hours. I would not advise rushing it any more than this.

Which method?

Just as there's more than one route to Rome, there is more than one way to get a beautiful slow-fermented sourdough loaf. In this book, I use two main methods—ambient and retarded. Each method produces loaves that taste slightly different from one another, and also, perhaps more importantly, have different levels of digestibility (see pages 188–189 for more on this). You need to choose which method in order to decide which leaven to make.

Choose ambient for a sweet loaf

Sometimes known as the "straight dough method", this is based on the way I was first taught to make bread in southwest France, in a village bakery built in 1750. It is the method I most often recommend to beginners, because it keeps you in touch with your dough. There were no fridges in the 18th century! Ambient method dough is mixed early in the morning, about 8 A.M., using leaven that had been left to ferment overnight. It has a relatively quick rise in a warm environment, and you bake your bread between 4–6 P.M., so it is ready for your supper.
It then makes wonderful toast the next day.
This method produces a less sour-flavored loaf.

Choose retarded for a sour & digestible loaf with higher nutrition

This method involves getting your dough fermenting, and then leaving it overnight to proof in the fridge, which slows down the yeast and allows the heterofermentative bacteria (which prefer lower temperatures) to get to work and produce acetic acid, giving the bread amazing sour, lightly vinegary flavors. It is the sourness that contributes to its digestibility. This method allows for more flexible timings. It is rather lovely to wake up on a Sunday morning, take your dough out of the fridge, preheat the oven while you have coffee and then put your bread into the oven. Alternatively, you can leave the dough in the fridge and bake it later in afternoon. For those who have wheat sensitivity, or digestive issues, it is also the method that allows for higher levels of acidity and therefore is more digestible as it can be extended to 48 hours without compromising the oven spring too much.

Schedule

The forums and social media are littered with complaints about sourdough formulas not working. Whereas most formulas are open to interpretation, those for sourdough are not. Sourdough is unforgiving, with variables between ambient temperature and enzyme activity of flour being two key reasons why so many bakers fail.

Being a good baker involves judging the flour, feeling the dough, and sensing it. This comes with experience, so while I have given a schedule, and guide to timings, I cannot emphasize enough that these are flexible. To get the most out of this book, you will need to bake each formula a few times to find the ideal timings for your flour and ambient temperature. Although the differences may only be subtle, they will be key to getting the kind of bread you want. Keeping a record of timings is how you get to understand what works for you. You can also compare methods side by side to see which one gives you the best result.

The following schedule is the one we use in the bakery classroom at the School, which usually has a temperature of 71–75°F during the day and 64–68°F at night. The blank schedules are for you to record your own timings. Even if you are a seasoned baker, this is a useful exercise, because the layers of complexity in the schedule are ever changing. It is not just the weather, but the flour too, that changes between seasons, and each year there is a new batch of flour, which will then need re-evaluating.

Schedule

STEP	AMBIENT	RETARDED
1. REFRESH STARTER For a white roller-milled flour starter or chocolate starter	**Day 1: 11 A.M.** But if you are going to work then 8 A.M. would be ok	**Day 1: 11 P.M.** Leave out on the side overnight
OR for a whole-wheat or rye starter	**Day 1: 5 P.M.**	**Day 1: 6 P.M.** Leave out on the side until 10 P.M., then refrigerate overnight
2. MAKE LEAVEN	**Day 1: 10–11 P.M.** (see page 91)	**Day 2: Between 8–10 A.M. depending on flour** (see page 93)
3. MIX & AUTOLYZE	**Day 2: 8 A.M.**	**Day 2: 12 P.M.**
4. CONTINUE WITH AUTOLYZE & MIX IN LEAVEN	**Day 2: 8.30 A.M.**	**Day 2: 12.30 P.M.**
5. ADD SALT—START BULK & STRETCH & FOLD	**Day 2: 11 A.M.**	**Day 2: 1–1.15 P.M.**
6. END BULK. LAST STRETCH & FOLD. ADD INCLUSIONS	**Day 2: 2 P.M.**	**Day 2: 3–3.30 P.M.**
7. SHAPE & BENCH TIME	**Day 2: 2 P.M.**	**Day 2: 3.30 P.M.**
8. FLOOR TIME (THIS IS ONLY USED IN RETARDED METHOD	**Day 2: 2.30 P.M.**	**Day 2: 4–5 P.M.**
FINAL PROOF	This is a continuation of floor time	**Day 3: Overnight in the fridge ideally at 46–48°F** However if your fridge is 41°F or below, leave the dough for another hour on final proof
9. SCORE		
10. BAKE	**Day 2: 4.30–6 P.M.**	**Day 3:** Bake anytime after 8 A.M. but ideally about 4 P.M.

Your loaf schedule

Formula ....

Date ....

Please photocopy this form or download new ones from sourdough.co.uk

STEP	DATE/TIME	DATE/TIME
1. REFRESH STARTER		
2. MAKE LEAVEN		
3. MIX & AUTOLYZE		
4. CONTINUE WITH AUTOLYZE & MIX IN LEAVEN		
5. ADD SALT – START BULK & STRETCH & FOLD		
6. END BULK. LAST STRETCH & FOLD. ADD INCLUSIONS		
7. SHAPE & BENCH TIME		
8. FLOOR TIME (THIS IS ONLY USED IN RETARDED METHOD		
FINAL PROOF		
9. SCORE		
10. BAKE		

Keeping a record

Many of my students feel frustrated when they get good results one day, and not another. However, when they ask me why their loaf hasn't turned out the way they want, they cannot remember the essential details that might help me suggest where they are going wrong; details that are especially crucial if they are baking just once a week. To avoid this, I recommend keeping a record of each bake. It helps to build up a pattern, which in turn helps you to understand how your sourdough behaves. Factors such as the kind of flour you use, the ambient temperature on the day, and the length of each stage, all affect the final loaf. The record form here has been designed to help you capture the details of your baking. As your notes accumulate, they will give you the information needed to identify anything not going according to plan, or to repeat your "best loaf ever."

FACTORS THAT CAN AFFECT YOUR BREAD

▶ The type of yeast that has colonized your starter

▶ The type of bacteria present

▶ Your choice of flour (percentage of whole-wheat, stone-ground, etc. that you use)

▶ The amount of starter you use—larger quantities ferment more quickly

▶ Wetter dough ferments faster

Sourdough loaf record

Please photocopy this form or download new ones from sourdough.co.uk

DATE
....

WHEN WAS YOUR STARTER LAST REFRESHED?
....

DID YOU MAKE A LEAVEN?
....

TIME THAT THE LEAVEN WAS ADDED
....

TOTAL WEIGHT OF LEAVEN IN GRAMS
....

AMBIENT TEMPERATURE OF THE ROOM
YOU ARE BAKING IN
....

WHICH BRAND OF FLOUR?
....

TYPE OF FLOUR i.e., whole-wheat/rye/spelt/white?
....

IS THE FLOUR STONE-GROUND OR ROLLER-MILLED?
....

WEIGHT OF FLOUR not including flour in the leaven
....

AMOUNT OF WATER not including water in the leaven

TEMPERATURE OF WATER
....

TIME THAT THE FLOUR AND WATER WERE MIXED
....

AUTOLYZE TIME
....

BULK FERMENTATION
....

THE NUMBER OF STRETCH & FOLDS
....

TIME OF SHAPING
....

TOTAL TIME PROOFING IN THE BANNETON
....

LOCATION OF FINAL PROOF IN THE BANNETON
....

AMBIENT TEMPERATURE OF WHERE
THE DOUGH IS PROOFING
....

OVEN TEMPERATURE
....

TIME BAKED

Scores of how happy you are with your loaf:

CRUST COLOR AND TEXTURE Marks out of 10 ....

HOW WAS THE CRUMB? Marks out of 10 ....
ie., how happy are you with the amount of holes and
texture of the interior of your bread?

FLAVOR Marks out of 10 ....

Notes

Tips before you start

People often ask me what the secret to baking amazing sourdough is. They expect advice on the choice of flour, or the optimal timings, but the truth is far simpler. So many of our instincts have been stifled and disconnected in life, and never more so than with food. Sourdough is a connector. It connects us to the earth, to the farmers, to the millers, to each other, and to ourselves. Our instincts are to cherish and create, to nurture and nourish. Baking sourdough is about using our instincts. It is about passion, rhythm, and intimacy, and baking great sourdough means trusting your sense of touch, smell, and taste. So to answer this question, the key occurs in the moment that you make that connection. You will know when it happens, because you will fall truly, madly, and deeply in love with your bread, and it will become part of you.

If you want to make your bread more digestible and nutritious, there are three main factors to consider. Firstly, choose either a whole-wheat or rye starter to create higher levels of acetic acid. There will still be lactic acid, but these hetero-fermentative starters produce more total acidity (titratable acid), which is a measure of the complete acid levels of the bread. Evidence suggests that the higher the level of acidity, the more broken down the flour, which is the key to increased digestibility and nutrition.

Take the time to build up the microbes in your starter. Following the methods outlined in the step-by-step, will create a robust microbial colony for better, more vigorous fermentation, and higher levels of organic acids, while maintaining crumb integrity (a nice risen loaf) as the bread ferments slowly.

Secondly, ferment for longer. The longer the bread is fermented, the better, so using the retarded method is best for optimal nutrition and digestibility.

Thirdly, choose whole-wheat flour, and blend it to provide the widest diversity of food and nutrients for your microbes. Industrial, roller-milled white flour limits the levels of nutrition, and to a large degree, flavor too. That said, it is excellent scaffolding for a lighter, more open crumb. However, the very fact that you are making your bread is amazing; so don't get too hung up on the nutrition. Experiment and make the kind of bread you love.

Although I cannot emphasize enough that whole-wheat formulas are nutritionally the best, if you have digestive issues, a drastic change in fiber can be a shock to the system. Start with the classic sourdough formula, with just 20% whole-wheat, and get used to it. You can increase the hydration and quantity of whole-wheat a bit at a time. Of course, if you are already a sourdough baker, and baking with whole-wheat, you can skip straight to the higher hydration and whole-wheat formulas.

A more highly hydrated dough facilitates more enzyme activity (enzymes break down the flour), and creates a more open crumb. Working with a wetter dough can be challenging at first. However, the results are spectacular, and have that real "wow" factor that no other bread can touch, so it is worth persevering. Be patient, and work through the book logically, starting with the basic formula.

What happens if my bread doesn't turn out well?

MY BREAD IS FLAT AND HEAVY

▶ This is typical of under-fermentation. It is likely that you have not refreshed your starter, (see page 83), or that you mistimed your leaven (see page 69) or used a different flour to the one I suggested.

▶ If all these were correct, and it is still flat and heavy, check the temperature you are bulking at.

▶ If your desired dough temperature was correct throughout the process, then give your bread another half hour bulk and observe the results.

▶ If you have checked all the above, then you have to go back to the basics. Check that your starter is lively. Look for bubbles, and signs of life.

▶ Check how much water you have added. Sometimes reducing water can hold back the fermentation, which may well be that your flour is more absorbent than the flour I have used in my formulas. If your dough is tight, and there is clearly lots of fermentation going on, then your flour might need a little more water.

▶ Make sure that you are bulking for long enough. Most bulk timings are between 3 and 5 hours, again depending on your flour and temperatures.

▶ If you are getting a heavy loaf using an ambient method, then double check that the flour in the leaven is right (see page 67), and go easy when shaping. Be firm, but light when handling the dough, as heavy-handed shaping reduces the openness of the crumb.

▶ Finally, insure that your oven is hot enough, and that you have baked in a cloche or a Dutch oven (see equipment, page 202). This makes a huge difference.

MY SOURDOUGH IS FLAT AND LIGHT – LIKE A FRISBEE

▶ This is typical of over-fermentation. There is almost a ripple as the dough folds and spreads. It's very frustrating but easy to correct.

▶ Check the kind of flour that you are using, and definitely check the timings in your starter refreshment (see page 83), and that the timings of the leaven are correct.

▶ Make sure you are using a thermometer to check your temperatures. You want the dough during bulk to be 79–82°F. You need to check your timings too. Make sure that you are keeping the autolyze short if you are using the retarded method.

▶ Check your fridge temperature if you are retarding overnight: 41°F is correct.

▶ It may very well be that your flour is more active, and you might want to shorten the bulk fermentation.

▶ Check that your base white flour is between 11–13% protein. Lower protein flours need less water.

▶ Double check your measurements. Too much water can also cause a loaf to be flat and unmanageable, or adding in all the water at once can have the same effect. The *bassinage* method insures that the gluten develops, and you don't flood your bread.

▶ Lastly, do make sure that you are using bread flour between 11 and 13%. Whole-wheat bread flour should be 11–13% and fresh: not more than 3 months old. That your base flour is a roller-milled 11–13% bread flour. If you are using a stone-ground flour, it will ferment faster, so you will need to adjust your timings and shorten the bulk.

Step-by-step
master method

How to refresh & maintain your starter to control flavor

First, you need to choose either the ambient or retarded (see page 70) method. Once you have your starter, you are ready to get going. Before you begin, you need to choose what kind of starter you want, based on what you want for your bread (see pages 84–87).

When it comes to starters, it is important to understand that different flours ferment at different rates, depending on the amount of enzymes and nutrients available to the microbes. Generally the wetter starters ferment faster, and are more lactic and sweeter, while thicker, lower hydration starters are more sour, as the acetic acid producing microbes favor more oxygen-rich environments.

White roller-milled flour that ferments at a moderate rate over 6 –8 hours gives an optimal microbial colony that is ready to make a leaven with. Rye is generally ready in about 3 hours, and whole-wheat in about 4 hours.

....

WHAT KIND OF FLOUR DO YOU RECOMMEND?
I recommend using organic flour, made if possible, from grain that has not been treated at any time with fungicides, herbicides, or artificial fertilizers; none of these agrochemicals belong in a starter. In short, use organic.

....

HOW OFTEN SHOULD I REFRESH?
At least once a week, and always the day before you make a leaven.

1. Refresh your starter

It is imperative before you start baking that you reactivate your starter, and build the microbial numbers. To do this you simply remove the "mother" from the fridge. She will be liquid and smell sour, but not unpleasant. Don't worry if there is a hooch on top, just stir it back in, or if it is very old, pour it away.

1. Put the starter from one of the formulas on pages 84–87 into a jug with the specified amount of water and whisk.

....

2. Discard the remaining starter (or keep this for the rye formula on page 127). Don't be tempted to use more, as it will acidify the new starter. Clean your pot thoroughly with hot water.

....

3. Pour in the milky-looking sourdough-inoculated water into the now clean pot, and stir in the flour. Mix well.

....

4. Leave the pot, loosely covered, in a cool, but not cold area, such as the kitchen worktop, over-night. This way the yeast and bacteria colonize the mixture, and it will be ready to make a leaven with when it is bubbly, has doubled in volume, and is full of life again. When your starter is at its microbial peak, it needs to go back into the fridge, covered, but not totally airtight. Please remember not to use every last bit when you bake, as you need some to build a new starter back up.

....

5. Choose your formula from pages 112–179 for the correct starter to use.

If you like a sweet loaf, choose between:

White starter
milky & sweet with a light tang
Encourages homofermentative LAB

....

This starter produces a very light-flavored French- style milky bread and it's one I was first introduced to in the French bakery when I was growing up. We use finely-milled organic white flour. The starter is kept at 100% hydration, meaning equal quantities of water to flour.

HOW TO REFRESH AND MAINTAIN
25g white starter (see page 62)
100g organic white flour
100g water at 96.8°F

Mix all the ingredients in a pot, leaving room for the starter to rise again by half. Cover with a breathable lid, and leave to ferment at an ambient temperature of 68–73°F for 8–10 hours. Ideally use immediately to make a leaven (see page 67). If that's not possible, refrigerate, and use to make a leaven within 8 hours. Refrigerate the remainder in a covered pot until next needed.

Refresh at least twice a week.

Chocolate starter
sweet & bitter

Encourages homofermentative LAB

This starter was made using the last chocolate bar my late friend and chocolatier Mott Green gave to me. I used the bar melted to start this culture as a way of always remembering him. It is bittersweet. I use raw cacao to refresh it, because cocoa beans, which are usually fermented with lactic acid bacteria in tropical heat under banana leaves, get hot, and the bacteria creates acidity in the same way as sourdough. Tropical temperatures are usually above 93°F, and studies show that there are some very interesting homofermentative LAB in raw cacao, plus, because it's not heat treated, it produces some really amazing flavors. We add 5% sugar to encourage osmotolerant yeast development. That simply means the yeasts resist osmosis (water being drawn out of them by sugar, which slows or stops fermentation) and so this starter is more robust when baking sweet sourdough.

HOW TO REFRESH AND MAINTAIN

Refresh at 100% hydration at 97°F, using fine white stone-ground flour, organic raw cacao powder, and organic sugar to create sweeter breads.

25g white starter (see page 62)
75g organic white flour
25g raw organic cacao powder
100g water at 97°F
10g organic raw cane sugar

Mix all the ingredients in a pot, leaving room for the starter to rise again by half. Cover with a breathable lid, and leave to ferment at an ambient temperature of 68–73°F for 8–10 hours. Ideally, use immediately to make a leaven (see page 67). If that's not possible, refrigerate and use to make a leaven within 8 hours. Refrigerate the remainder in a covered pot until next needed.

Refresh at least twice a week minimum, and 8–12 hours before you make a leaven.

HOW TO REFRESH AND MAINTAIN

This starter is kept at 70% hydration—reducing the amount of water enables more oxygen for the heterofermentative bacteria, which they favor—and refreshed with water at a temperature of 59–64°F. It has a fabulous sharp tang to it, and we cultivate the heterofermentative bacteria with the lower water temperature and British whole-wheat flour to get a really good sourness.

25g whole-wheat starter
100g organic whole-wheat flour
  (preferably from Britain or Northern Europe)
70g water at 59–64°F

Mix all the ingredients in a pot, leaving room for the starter to rise again by half. Cover with a breathable lid, and leave to ferment at an ambient temperature of 68–73°F for 5–6 hours. Ideally use immediately to make a leaven (page 67). If that's not possible, refrigerate and use to make a leaven within 8 hours. Refrigerate the remainder in a covered pot until next needed.

Refresh twice a week, and 4 hours before you make a leaven.

If you like a sour loaf, choose between:

Whole-wheat starter
a sweet & sour loaf that is easier to digest
Encourages heterofermentative LAB

Our whole-wheat starter started life in the iconic Tartine Bakery in San Francisco. It makes beautiful, tender, tangy sourdough. When a small pot arrived 5,000 miles back at the School we analyzed the LAB.
Lactobacillus sanfrancisensis
Lb. acidophilus
Lb. pentosus
Lb. pontis

It was still wonderfully sweet and lactic. It had been kept on a frequent 115% hydration refreshment schedule, and had been used to being refreshed four times a day. I already had my white starter, but only having one starter limited the flavors I could produce, so I decided to change this one, and use it as the base for our whole-wheat starter. Keeping up the four times a day refreshment schedule was impossible, and I wanted to use British flour, so I reduced the hydration to 60%, making it a stiff starter and reduced the refreshment schedule to three times a week. A year later I wanted to know what had changed. The starter had retained three out of four of the LAB and lost the lowest bacteria *Lb. pontis*. It also gained two more in the pot
Lactobacillus kimchii
Lactobacilli brevis
I am certain these came from the kimchii already established in my white starter and the milk kefir in the fridge in the School.

Rye starter
tangy, sour, & fruity
with good digestibility

Encourages heterofermentative LAB

....

I made this rye starter with Norwegian baker
Martin Fjeld from Ille Brød. It is fabulously
tangy and acidic, and is the one I use most
often if I want to bake in a hurry—the higher
levels of enzymes and sugars in rye, especially
when using milled fresh flour, mean that it
ferments fast. We refresh with freshly-ground
rye flour using a small mill.

HOW TO REFRESH AND MAINTAIN

Like the whole-wheat starter, this is kept as a stiff
starter, which increases the amount of oxygen
available, so favoring the heterofermentative
bacteria—and refreshed with water at 59°F.

25g rye starter
100g organic rye flour
  (preferably from Britain or Northern Europe)
70g water at 59°F

Mix all the ingredients in a pot, leaving room
for the starter to rise again by half. Cover with a
breathable lid, and leave to ferment at an ambient
temperature of 68–73°F for 3–4 hours. Ideally
use immediately to make a leaven (see page 70
for the retarded method). If that's not possible,
refrigerate, and use to make a leaven within 8
hours. Refrigerate the remainder in a covered pot
until next needed.

Refresh twice a week, and 3–5 hours before you
make your leaven.

Ready to use

HOW DO I KNOW IF MY STARTER IS RIPE AND READY TO BAKE WITH?

It will have risen by about double, be bubbly, smell lightly and pleasantly of yogurt, and float in water, if a small amount is tested.

WHAT ABOUT THE LEFTOVER STARTER?

Once you have used 25 grams of starter, the rest is discarded. I don't throw it away though—no one likes to waste food! I keep it in a separate pot in the fridge and add to waffles, scones (biscuits), and pancakes, formulas which are on our website. There is, however, one very distinctive formula that uses up the discard—the Russian rye bread on page 127—it uses 700 grams of discarded sourdough starter. The Sourdough powders on pages 45–46 are another wonderful way to recycle fermented starter.

WHY KEEP SO MUCH STARTER IN THE FIRST PLACE?

I'm often asked this question, but it comes down to experience. I have noticed that smaller amounts of starter spoil more easily. About 200–250 grams is an optimal amount for a home baker. I cannot offer a scientific explanation for this, just many years of observation, and seeing starters brought to me in clinics at the School, show that 250 grams is a critical mass for ideal microbial health.

WHITE LEAVEN FOR AMBIENT METHOD: READY IN 6–8 HOURS

2. Make your leaven
the foundation of your dough

You can use any starter to make a leaven. The thing that really matters is that it has a robust community of microbes that have been recently refreshed.

The following timings are based on the ambient temperature in the School classroom, which is 68–73°F.

Leaven using the ambient method

For the ambient method, I suggest using white flour, as it ferments at a slightly slower rate than whole-wheat or rye, and so will be ready to use in 7–9 hours. It will still be usable for an additional 2 hours, enabling you to mix your leaven, get a good night's sleep, and use first thing in the morning.

25g sourdough starter
100g strong white bread flour
90g water at 79°F

RYE AND WHOLE-WHEAT LEAVEN FOR RETARDED METHOD:
READY IN 2–4 HOURS

Leaven using the retarded method

I suggest you use either rye or whole-wheat flours, as they are generally faster fermenting, because they contain more enzymes and nutrients. Either of these flours will make a leaven that will be ready in about 2–4 hours. It will also be usable for an additional 2 hours, though this is not ideal.

25g sourdough starter
100g rye or whole-wheat flour
100g water at 86°F

Mixing

Let me start by saying that all the loaves in this book were hand-mixed. Perhaps my favorite part of the process is when I actually get my hands into the flour and water, and feel the dough coming together. It is important to get mixing right, as it is a crucial part of baking, and an aspect that many home bakers overlook. At the School, I teach how to mix by hand, which for domestic bakers, is very much part of experiencing the sensory nature of baking. I encourage people to feel the dough and become familiar with the way the flour hydrates. Getting to know the feel of it as it comes together, helps you to understand how the flour behaves.

The speed and length of the mixing is integral to the success of the final loaf. The mixing develops the gluten, so affects the structure of the loaf. If the mixing time or speed is misjudged, the texture and the grain of the crumb can be compromised. To get uniformity of dough, you have to put in just the right amount of energy to mix the water and the flour, and develop the gluten.

I recommend mixing using a lot of energy. You will develop some good muscles over time. You can also stretch and fold the dough once the flour and water are incorporated. Using a mixer will give you a stronger gluten network, however all the breads in this book were hand-mixed.

If you want to mix larger amounts of dough, I recommend using a mixer with a spiral action. This is better for dough development because it gently mixes the dough without overworking it. The bowl of the mixer rotates as the spiral hook is spinning to knead the dough. This means that the spiral hook is kneading only a portion of the whole dough mass, which keeps friction-generated heat low, and results in a consistent mix. This is really important, because if the temperature of the dough isn't right, it will affect the rate of fermentation, which in turn affects the volume of the bread, and the color of the crust.

A good mixer needs to be heavy and robust so it stays put while weighty dough is being tossed around. It will also have multiple speeds to give the baker more control over the dough development. Low speed helps bring the mix together into a homognous mass. The higher speeds are used in short bursts of rest/mix for between 8–20 minutes, depending on the amount of dough, and the temperature as the salt goes in to develop the gluten structure of the dough. When using a mixer, you need to take into account the likelihood of friction raising the dough temperature, and adjust the water temperature accordingly.

3. Mix the dough

1. When your leaven is ready to use, it will be bubbly, fresh, and smell similar to live yogurt.

....

2. When you first mix, it is essential not to add all the water in at once. You mix in just 70% of the water from the formula for white and about 80% for whole-wheat.

Set the remaining water aside as this water is going in, but not yet (see page 42 for water advice)!

....

3. Add the water and leaven to a warmed mixing bowl. You can add more water later, but it is important that it is the correct temperature, as this will determine the speed of fermentation. The initial dough temperature needs to be 82°F for optimal yeast development. In winter, I use water at 91°F as the temperature drops when I first mix. In summer, I reduce the water temperature to 73–79°F depending on the warmth of the day. If you are in a hot country, you will need to reduce the water temperature further still.

....

4. Whisk well to get rid of any lumps and incorporate air.

....

5. Add the flour.

....

6. Mix well for a couple of minutes, insuring that all the flour is incorporated. This mixing encourages the gluten to develop. Stop mixing for step 4 to autolyze, then you will continue mixing at step 5 when the salt is added. It is really important that you rest for a few minutes between mixing to develop the gluten.

4. Autolyze

This refers to the period of rest after the initial mixing of flour and water, which allows the flour to absorb water without the inhibiting presence of salt. It gives the gluten and starches the chance to form, which leads both to better dough development and better flavor. Breads made with autolyzed dough are easier to shape, and have more volume and improved structure. There is a short autolyze for the retarded method, and a longer one for the ambient. A true autolyze occurs without the addition of leaven. At the School we autolyze for 20 minutes without leaven, but pre-salt. Then we add the leaven, and continue the second part of the autolyze without salt. I regard the addition of the salt as the end of the autolyze. I've heard this step referred to as "fermentolyze", but for simplicity, since most bakers around the world agree that this term has evolved from its original definition, it is referred to as autolyze.

TYPES OF AUTOLYZE

1 Pure autolyze or pre-leaven. Traditional French bakers mix just flour and water.
2 Autolyze with leaven. Most formulas call for this technique.

WHY DO WE HAVE A PRE-LEAVEN AUTOLYZE?

Pre-leaven is the stage when the mixing takes place. Mixing develops the gluten, and it is best to do this without any acidity from the leaven.

WHAT TEMPERATURE DOES THE DOUGH NEED TO BE DURING AUTOLYZE?

▶ By hand: keep the bowl covered with a wet dish towel. The warm water should keep the dough at 82°F initially, but it is best not to allow the temperature to drop much below 73°F.
▶ By machine: 68–72°F.

HOW DO I KEEP THE TEMPERATURE CONSTANT?

You need to use a thermometer to measure, and you can either use a bread proofer such as a Brød & Taylor, or sit the mixing bowl in a large dishpan, and top up regularly with warm water. Alternatively, put the bowl, covered, into the oven with just the pilot light on. What matters is that you keep dough at its optimal fermentation temperature (between 73 and 82°F). Do not be tempted to go warmer: more heat is not better!

WHY DON'T BAKERIES DO THIS?

Most bakeries are warmer environments than domestic kitchens, and they ferment a lot of dough which self insulates.

SO HOW DOES IT WORK?

During the autolyze, the flour absorbs the water, becoming fully hydrated. This activates enzymes in the flour that stimulate the proteins to start gluten development. At the same time, other enzymes are starting to break starch down into the simple sugars that will feed the yeast during the bulk proof. These two processes would happen during traditional dough-making, but importantly, during autolyze they are happening before any kneading is done, and the total amount of kneading is reduced. Too much kneading can result in an over-oxidized dough, which detracts from the finished bread's color, flavor, and texture.

Like many aspects of breadmaking, the autolyze technique is used in different ways by different bakers. The length of time allowed varies—usually between 30 minutes and 2 hours is recommended. The length of the autolyze will affect the amount of stretching and folding required once the leaven and salt are added. I generally find that bread made with stone-ground flour improves with a longer autolyze. This is because the extra moisture, coupled with the stone-ground milling process, means that the flour has larger starch particles, which means that it absorbs the water more slowly. Autolyze gives the flour the chance to hydrate, and the proteins have the opportunity to bond before the dough is handled, which makes the most of the gluten present.

WHY DO WE TEND TO AUTOLYZE WITH LEAVEN AT THE SCHOOL?

Mainly because I have seen no visible difference between autolyzing before and after adding leaven. This is because we hand mix, which makes it easier to distribute the leaven evenly when adding it in with the water in the initial mixing, and because of the long fermentation times. Occasionally, we autolyze without leaven, for example in the baguette and rye formulas.

WHAT ABOUT THE SALT?

Adding the salt marks the end of the autolyze. It is never added until this stage because it tightens the gluten network. You can feel this effect when you mix salt into the dough—it becomes harder to stretch out during kneading. You are looking to develop the extensibility of the dough during autolyze, and adding the salt before this stage is complete would work against this.

Autolyze: what, why, & how

Autolyze is a deceptively simple process that can be easily introduced into your breadmaking routine. It delivers a dough that's easier to work with and to shape, and a loaf with better texture, rise, and flavor. Just combine the flour and water in a bowl, and mix until no dry flour remains. Do not be tempted to knead. Cover the bowl, and leave it in a warm place for anything from 20 minutes to up to 3 hours. During this time, gluten development begins, and simple sugars start to form as starch is broken down. Although it may look like nothing is happening, you will notice the difference as soon as you handle the dough, because during the autolyze, it will have become smoother and more elastic.

Professor Raymond Calvel introduced the technique in his book *Le Gout du Pain* (published in English as *The Taste of Bread*). He was a research chemist who pretty much single-handedly transformed French breadmaking. It's hard to imagine now, but despite its long history of excellence, after the Second World War, the quality of French bread was in decline. Calvel, who trained many well-known bakers and cooks, including American chef Julia Child, focused on finding ways to improve the flavor and character of French bread. His experiments revealed that mixing flour and water, then allowing this mixture to stand before adding yeast and salt, reduced the total mixing and kneading time required. This resulted in bread that has a creamy crumb and good flavor.

5. Add salt
for flavor & strength

Your autolyzed dough should show bubbles and signs of life. This is also the step where you add miso, soy, or seaweed if they are included in the formula.

1. Sprinkle the salt evenly over the dough and mix in.

2. Use 25g from the total water and evenly distribute across the surface to integrate the salt. Mix well, first by dimpling your fingers into the dough, then by pushing your hand in and twisting, mimicking the movement of a mixer. Do this for 2–3 minutes until the salt is fully incorporated. You will feel the gluten developing as you do this. This is now ready for the bulk fermentation.

EAU DE BASSINAGE

One of the questions people always ask is how they can open up the crumb structure of their bread. One of the ways you can do this is to incrementally add water. Once your gluten is developed, you need to add in the remaining water a little at a time. This technique is known in France as *"eau de bassinage."*

The remaining water is mixed into the dough incrementally 20g at a time. Mix, then rest for a minute. If the dough looks saturated, wait a couple of minutes.

Once all but the last 45g of water has been incorporated, sprinkle the salt evenly over the dough, and use about 25g of the water. Mix in, and continue to mix to develop the gluten. The last saved 20g of water is best saved for the stretch and fold.

RETARDED SALT TECHNIQUE

▶ Mix the salt in well. When I am mixing on a machine, I mix for 3 minutes, rest for 5 minutes, then repeat three times after the salt is added.
▶ Once the gluten is developing, you will feel the dough tighten. Leave it for a couple of minutes to relax.
▶ Then start adding in the rest of the water using a *bassinage*.
▶ The dough is now ready for bulk.

AMBIENT SALT TECHNIQUE

▶ This is a gentler technique. We aim to mix the salt in, but without losing too much volume.
▶ The *bassinage* water is added incrementally and the last 20–30g is worked in during the bulk stretch and fold.

6. Bulk fermentation
stretch and fold

1. You now leave your dough to ferment, during which time you will need to stretch and fold it, which helps to give your bread structure.

2. How to stretch and fold

Instead of traditional kneading, we teach a stretch and fold technique. This helps the gluten in the dough to develop. During the bulk fermentation, you need to stretch and fold the dough in the bowl three separate times at evenly spaced intervals. Each stretch consists of four or five folds at a time. To do a fold, dip one hand in water to prevent sticking (or use a really light olive oil). Shake off the excess water. Grab the underside of the dough, stretch it out, and fold it back over itself. Rotate the bowl a quarter turn, and stretch and fold more of the dough. Do this rotate, stretch and fold two or three more times, then stop. It is important to be progressively gentle each time, so as not to lose volume.

Inclusions Add fruit, nuts, and seeds inclusions on the last but one set of stretch and folds.

Porridge Add porridge on the second set of stretch and folds. It is often not completely incorporated, leaving something of a thin marble-like effect, but this is fine.

3. At the end of the bulk fermentation the dough should feel firm and aerated. There should be a 50% increase in volume for the retarded, and 60% increase for ambient. If you cut it open, you should be able to see bubbles. If not, continue fermentation for an additional 30 minutes to an hour or so.

If you are baking using the ambient method, you need only preshape

7. Shaping your loaf
create the scaffolding

There is one main distinction when shaping the dough between the ambient method and the retarded method. For ambient, it only needs a light preshape. For retarded, it must have more strength for the longer proof time, so the dough needs a second shape to tension it.

1. If you are new to handling dough, a drop of oil on your hands will help create a natural barrier. Lightly flour both your dough and the work surface. (If you have digestive sensitivities, use rice or potato flour, or sourdough powder, see page 45). Turn out your dough onto the work surface. Divide into the number of loaves specified in the formula you are following. You can either do this by eye, or if you are unsure and prefer to be exact, by adding together the weight of the ingredients in the formula, and dividing by the number of loaves to give you an exact weight. Using a scraper to cut through the dough, stretch out each piece very gently to the size of a small dinner plate. Apply the following steps to both pieces of dough.

....

2. With your scraper at an angle of 45 degrees, scrape under the dough. This loosens it from the work surface making the next step easy. Place your left-hand index finger in the center, and working your way clockwise around the dough, fold in the corners to form a tight boule (round) shape. Once you have a boule, flip it over. All the joins are on the bottom now. Be gentle, but firm with your dough when you are shaping.

Being gentle but firm, work each piece into a round by using the scraper, still at 45 degrees, and your hand. The dough will stick slightly to the surface as you rotate and drag it. The aim is to create an even tightness and tension that becomes the crust. When it is nicely structured, it will hold itself together. This takes time and practice. (There are also videos of this step online.)

....

3. BENCH REST

You must now bench rest the dough for 20 minutes or so to give the gluten time to relax. You put in the final structure on the next shape. If you are baking using the ambient method, this step is not strictly necessary.

4. Once your dough has bench rested, it's ready for its final shaping. (Following static pictures in a book is perhaps the most challenging way to try and learn to shape.)

If you are making a boule, dust a seasoned banneton well with flour or sourdough powder (see page 45) to stop the dough from sticking.

Any coatings, such as malt flakes or seeds, can be added at this point by scattering them on a large plate, and rolling the top of the dough (i.e., the surface that is going to be facing down in the banneton) over the plate. You can then transfer any that are not used back into the jar.

Slip your scraper beneath the dough and lift it, being careful to maintain the shape. Place the dough seam-side up in the pre-floured banneton for the second shape retarded method. DO NOT dust the top with flour. Leave the dough for 10 minutes for the gluten to relax.

Stitching
You can further tighten the dough by pulling pieces from the outer edge into the middle. The natural behavior of the dough is to stick to itself, and so this creates more tension. This is a brilliant trick to increase the strength on the final shape, and especially useful if you are new to shaping. Pulling the dough simultaneously from opposite sides of the banneton is actually the same principle as lacing a boot, creating equal tension on each side. By the end of your shaping, the dough should have a taut outer membrane that will give you a superb classic sourdough crust.

If you are making a batard
Follow the instructions for shaping a boule, but, once the boule is shaped, place both hands on the boule, and roll it backwards and forwards with pressure moving the dough away from the center to create pointed ends.

Place the boule batard with the seam side down on a floured *couche* (similar to page 149). Proof until ready to bake.

8. Proof
increase the volume

For the retarded method

FLOOR TIME

This step is for the retarded method only. In the ambient method, there is just one final proofing, but in the retarded method, this is the chance for bakers to give the dough some time to continue fermenting at a higher temperature before it goes into the fridge. Depending on how fast or slow the fermentation is, and the ambient temperature of your kitchen or bakery, this can be anything from 20 minutes to an hour. It takes time to get to understand how the dough behaves, and each formula is different, but the purpose is to give the dough a final proof at ambient temperature. Once this is completed, the dough is ready for the final proof in the fridge overnight.

FINAL PROOF

Give the top of the dough a very light dusting of flour, cover with a clean dish towel, and transfer to the fridge for the final proof overnight. Ideally, it should be set to a temperature of 46–48°F. Professional bakeries have proofers that can be set to this temperature, but for health and safety reasons, domestic fridges are normally set to 41°F or lower. If it's not possible for you to have a separate fridge in which to ferment your bread, and you are using a domestic one, find the warmest spot using a fridge thermometer. This is often at the top, at the front, though not if you have an ice-making compartment here. The biggest input of heat is the warm air that rushes in each time you open the door. As cold air sinks, it collects at the bottom. Frost-free fridges tend to circulate the air, and have much more even temperature distribution. If your dough has not risen sufficiently, it will be because the fridge is too cold, so you might need to extend the floor time.

It is worth noting that if you want to achieve the maximum breakdown of proteins—which is important for anyone with suspected wheat sensitivity—you can leave your loaf for an additional 12–24 hours. The compromise is 10–20% less oven spring, however this is of little concern for people who need maximum digestibility.

For the ambient method

There is no floor time needed for this method. Confusing, I know, but the dough is already on the side! You simply leave it to continue to proof in the ambient temperature of the room (this is the final proof for this method). In the summer when it is warm, or with higher hydration dough, you can place the dough in the coldest part of the fridge for 30 minutes to an hour to cool it down at the end of this proof. The advantage of this is that cold dough is far easier to score, and generally gets a slightly better oven spring.

How to tell if your dough is ready to bake

The golden question. You have built an army of microbes, built the dough structure, shaped it and built tension, and proofed it. Is it ready? The strange thing is that knowing if it is ready is actually about getting to know your dough. I can't teach experience, only practice will give you the understanding of how each nuance affects the dough's readiness. That said, there are indicators that the dough is ready. It will have increased in size, generally by about 50%. The gluten is a series of elastic air pockets that have caught the air like balloons. You need there to be some tension still in the dough. A typical mistake a beginner makes, is to push this point as far as possible, thinking that the more air the better. The dough actually needs to have somewhere still to expand to as it goes in the oven, or the "elastic" gluten will be weak, acidified, and over-extended, and it will ripple as you turn it out and deflate. The opposite is true if you underproof. The dough will be heavy as there is no air in the gluten network, and your loaf will be dense.

You will need to stay close to your dough, and get a sense of it coming alive. Look for texture and small bubbles. Look for an increase in volume. The more you do this, the better you will become at judging whether it is ready. Once the bread is in the banneton, you can check the last stages by touching the dough. As a general guide:

▶ **if it springs straight back when pressed, it is immature. It needs longer.**
▶ **if it answers you back in a considered way, gently and evenly, it is ready to bake.**
▶ **if it is very puffed up and you leave a fingerprint in the dough, it is bordering on overproofed.**
▶ **if it completely deflates when you press it, it is overproofed.**

If the dough is overproofed and you feel like bursting into tears, don't completely despair. You rescue it by transferring it to a tray, dimpling the surface and throwing over 150ml olive oil, 6–8 garlic cloves, a tablespoon of coarse sea salt and a large handful of rosemary sprigs in and around the dough—it will pass as a very respectable focaccia. Note down your timings in your loaf record sheet, and adjust accordingly. For overproofed dough, reduce the timings, and for underproofed, increase them.

9. Score
score and bake

I've separated scoring into its own step, but really this is a split-second movement literally moments before the bread goes into the oven. Scoring your loaf is not actually essential, but understanding the effect of scoring is key to getting a more open- and better-structured loaf.

In the heat of the oven, the dough expands. By scoring you give the bread the opportunity to expand freely. Making shallow cuts results in a more open crumb, and a beautiful pattern in the bread, and if you get it right, you get a much-coveted "ear." This is more pronounced on oval or long loaves.

The success of the score depends on many factors: the tension that you build as you shape, the integrity of the gluten, which depends on the bread being perfectly proofed, the sharpness of your blade, the speed and angle that you cut at, and the ear that forms is also dependent on there being enough steam around the bread as it bakes, and finally, it is dependent on the oven temperature being correct. If your oven goes to 450°F, then this is the best temperature to use. I have recommended to bake at 425°F as most ovens can reach this. Keep the second loaf in the fridge while the first one bakes.

HOW TO SCORE

▶ Use a *lame*, never a kitchen knife as these are not sharp enough.

▶ Relax, but once you score, get your dough straight into the oven. To begin with, start with a single cut, with the *lame*, made in one smooth movement using the blade at a 45 degree angle down the bread. Think of a surgeon at work. Not a tree surgeon—no sawing motions! I recommend you turn your bread out with the shortest end facing you. I like to score slightly to one side (I prefer the right but I am right-handed,) and slightly curved, moving with the natural curve of the bread. Start at the top of the dough and bring the blade toward you. Under NO circumstances do you put your hand in the way, and pressing on the dough deflates it. It's one movement.

▶ Once you have mastered this you can do a Picasso if you want, personally I only rarely score a fancy pattern, as each cut de-flates the delicate gluten network you have built. It takes practice to get it right, and even after so many years of baking, I occasion-ally get it wrong some days.

SCORE AND GET STRAIGHT INTO THE OVEN

10. Bake
heat and steam

1. About 45 minutes before your bread is ready to bake, preheat your oven to 450°F (or 475°F if your oven will go that high) and place a La Cloche baking dome or Dutch oven in it to get hot.

2. If baking a boule, once your oven has reached 450°F, carefully remove your cloche or Dutch oven, making sure not to burn yourself, and, if using a cloche, generously dust the base (inside) with polenta or semolina. If using a Dutch oven, tear off 16 inches of baking parchment, and use it to lower the dough into the pot. Once the lid is on, you can trim the paper to size, but remember to leave enough length to get the bread out of the pot once it has been baked.

3. Take one of your loaves out of the fridge. Carefully remove the lid of your cloche or Dutch oven, and turn the dough out onto the hot base, taking care not to burn yourself. Score (see page 108). If you are someone who struggles to do this, a couple of snips with very sharp scissors is a good alternative. If you don't do this, the dough will split anyway, so by scoring it, you decide where the bread expands, and can better control its shape.

4. Once your bread is in the oven, reduce the temperature to 350°F, but do check each formula, as some have specific baking temperatures, depending on the inclusions. Bake for 1 hour. After this time, remove the lid, and continue baking the loaf for an additional 5 minutes or so, until the crust is a deep golden brown—use your judgement, it can be longer if you like a darker crust.

5. Remove the loaf from the pot, and transfer it to a wire rack to cool. In this moment your bread should be glorious. It will feel light, and the crust will be burnished with a range of beautifully rich golden copper and mahogany colors. My sourdough rarely hangs about for long, but it is best stored wrapped in linen or cotton, and the sourness actually improves with age. Eat within 1 week.

If you only have one cloche or Dutch oven, repeat from step 1 with your second loaf (it is advisable to keep it in the fridge until you bake it, or it may overproof).

HOW LONG DO I NEED TO BAKE FOR?

I recommend that you bake your loaf for 1 hour, and then remove the lid and continue baking for an additional 5 minutes or so until the crust is a deep golden brown. However, what is right for one person, is not right for another. It can be longer if you like a darker crust, or a few minutes shorter if you like a lighter crust.

WHY IS IT SO IMPORTANT TO USE A DUTCH OVEN, LODGE PAN, OR CLOCHE?

Many people just use a baking stone to bake their bread, but using a cast-iron Dutch oven, Lodge pan, or a La Cloche baking dome makes the difference between a good loaf and a great one. Domestic ovens are not great for baking bread. They are temperamental, and have hot spots, and the heat is usually from one direction. Often the seals are not airtight, and they have drafts. They also dry the crust out too fast. Putting the lid on your cloche or Dutch oven means that the steam let off by the bread as it bakes is trapped. This steam is fantastic at keeping the crust soft, which allows the dough to expand. It is also very forgiving if your oven is fierce.

WHAT HAPPENS AS YOUR LOAF COOLS?

When a baked loaf starts cooling, the starch changes from a chaotic to crystalline structure—the granules link together, which gradually changes the jelly-like crumb straight from the oven to a firmer texture that we like to eat as bread. This reaction continues until ultimately the crumb becomes cold as the water evaporates. It then begins to turn stale.

What happens in the oven?

DOUGH TEMPERATURE	EFFECT
68–113°F	When your sourdough is placed in the oven, it quickly rises in temperature, taking the yeast to its optimum for gas production. This is the beginning of the "oven jump."
131–140°F	The "thermal death point" occurs at 113–122°F. Both the lactic acid bacteria and the yeast die. Most of the oven spring has happened by this point.
140–158°F	At 140°F the gluten network denatures and breaks apart, releasing the water it is holding. This is the end of the "oven jump" because the gluten network breaks apart, and the gas starts to escape. At this temperature, the starch in the dough sucks up the released water and gelatinizes. Gelatinization is the starch granule that swells by the absorption of water and explodes. This means that the starch chains inside the starch granule start leaking out.
158–176°F	By this stage, the loaf has been in the oven for almost 20 minutes, and the bread shape is pretty much formed. Amylase activity decreases, and the gluten is denaturized fully.
176–194°F	The gelatinization of starch stops at 194°F.
194–212°F	212°F is the boiling point of water. Steam escapes, maximum internal dough temperature is reached, and the crust begins to color.
212–347°F	This is the magic point of flavor as ketones and aldehydes (organic compounds) form, and while a considerable amount evaporates during baking, they contribute significantly to the irresistible smell and flavour of freshly baked bread. This is also the zone where the Maillard reaction takes place.
347–450°F	There is continuation of the Maillard reaction, and caramelization of the crust. This is also the point at which, according to a German study, an antioxidant called Pronyl-lysine is formed by the reaction of the protein-bound amino acid L-lysine. This is a potential cancer-preventing antioxidant bread that is eight times more abundant in the dark crust than in the crumb.

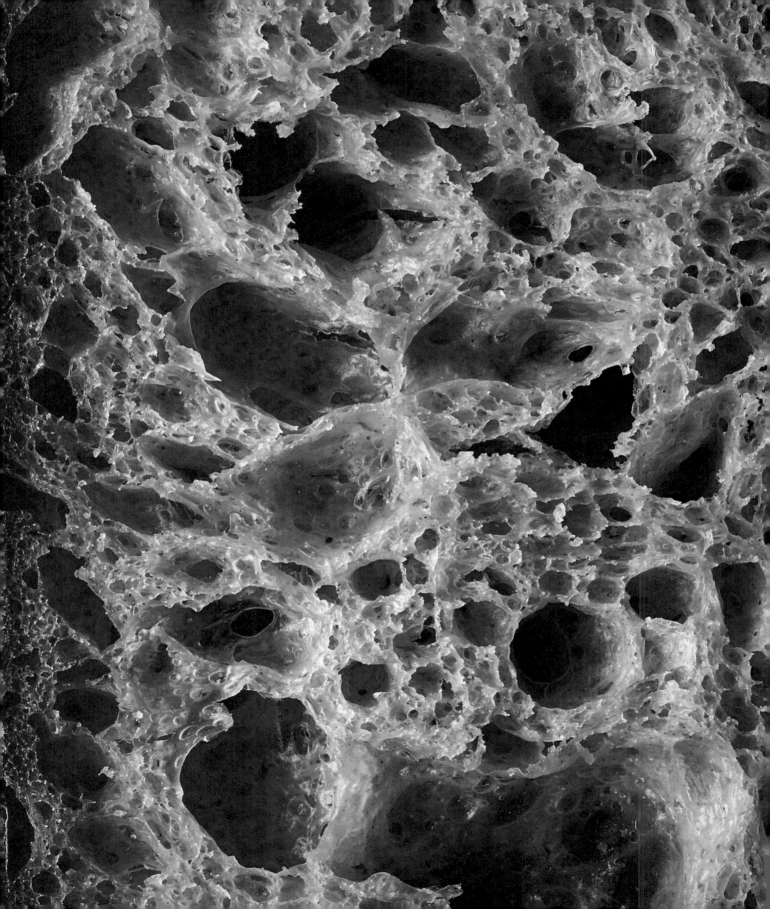

Formulas

Classic white sourdough boules

❯ INGREDIENTS

225g leaven (see pages 90–93)
735g water for the dough
800g white bread flour
200g stone-ground whole-wheat flour
5g diastatic malt powder (see page 51), optional
20g fine sea salt

❯ **SUGGESTED STARTER** Any starter as long as it is active will give you great bread, but if you want a tangy loaf, use a rye or whole-wheat starter. If you prefer a sweet, light-flavored loaf, use a homofermentative white or chocolate starter. See page 83 for instruction on starters.

❯ **SUGGESTED LEAVEN** Choose according to method (see pages 90–93).

❯ **SUGGESTED METHOD** When you first bake, I recommend you use the ambient method (see page 70). Sometimes called a "straight dough method", meaning that there is no retarding, it's a great way to learn, gives you a light-flavored loaf, and you stay connected to the dough all day. However, you can use whichever method you prefer according to your taste and schedule.

❯ **BEFORE YOU BEGIN** Make sure you read the **Step-by-step chapter** (page 80), and use both a dough schedule to plan your **timings** (see page 72), and a **loaf record sheet** to assess your bread (page 75).

This is the School's classic sourdough formula, the one we use to teach beginners, as it gives reliable results and helps build confidence. It's made with predominantly white flour and 20% stone-ground whole-wheat flour, which means that although it's perfect for learning the basics, it doesn't reach the full nutritional or flavor potential of a sourdough loaf. It is, however, the easiest one to handle to learn the techniques I teach. I recommend you bake it at least 5–7 times to get a feel for the timings before you move on to other formulas—familiarity will give you a better understanding of the process—and that you try all three methods to see which one suits you best.

Try to use the same flour each time to begin with, as this will help you to recognize the nuances of the dough as the seasons change. What might appear to be pretty subtle differences become more noticeable as you improve as a baker. With time, you will notice that the dough feels slightly different with each batch that you bake. Once you have become familiar with this formula, move on to a formula that uses more whole-wheat flour.

Advice

❯ The white bread flour we recommend is roller-milled and generally between 11 and 13% protein, which is considered a middle range of flour strength. (Flour bags that do not have stone-ground written on them are generally roller-milled flour, and you can get this kind of flour from almost any good store.)
❯ Remember to reserve water from the total for when you add the salt.
❯ The addition of diastatic malt is optional. It adds color and flavor, as well as extra enzymes, which convert the starches into sugar for the microbes to use, and is useful when using refined roller-milled white flour, but not stone-ground white.

Classic sourdough higher hydration

› INGREDIENTS

225g leaven (see pages 90–93)
825g water for the dough
800g white bread flour
200g stone-ground whole-wheat flour (11.5)
10g non-diastatic malt
20g fine sea salt

› SUGGESTED STARTER White or whole-wheat

› SUGGESTED METHOD Retarded

Advice

▶ Depending on the ambient temperature and the flour, you may need to reduce the bulk fermentation times by 10–15 minutes, as wetter dough has more enzyme activity and therefore proofs faster.

▶ Higher protein flours take more water, and lower protein ones less, but it is worth bearing in mind that lower protein flour also rewards the baker with more tender crumb structure.

▶ If you are a beginner and struggling, you may halve the amount of *bassinage* water and discard it.

Once you have mastered the classic sourdough boules on page 114, you might start to wonder how you can get larger holes—what bakers refer to as a more open crumb structure. This is achieved through minor changes to several factors in the basic formula, including mixing well in the beginning to develop the gluten, and adding more water. So this is the higher hydration version of the basic loaf.

Generally, the more water you add, the more open the crumb. A common phrase you will hear bakers using is "the wetter, the better." This is not strictly true, as you can over-hydrate flour and end up with a sloppy batter. To avoid this, it is best to add more water just a little at a time. The French term for this is *bassinage*. There isn't a direct English translation, but it means water that is worked into the dough in small increments during the bulk fermentation. A traditional technique, it involves setting aside some of the water and mixing the dough slightly firm in the first place. By doing this you develop the gluten in a stiffer dough and then "let it down" with the remaining water. Many domestic bakers misunderstand and add additional water, and it is a disaster. You will likely get flour soup!

So please, take note! The water is reserved from the total, and added in later.

Classic 50:50 whole-wheat/white sourdough boule

❯ INGREDIENTS

225g leaven (see pages 90–93)
850g water for the dough
500g strong white roller-milled flour
500g stone-ground whole-wheat flour
20g fine sea salt

❯ SUGGESTED STARTER White or whole-wheat, or rye

❯ SUGGESTED METHOD Retarded

Advice

▶ Keep in mind that the more whole-wheat flour there is, the faster the dough ferments. This is especially noticeable when using British or northern European flours, as in a maritime climate, grains tend to have higher levels of enzymes than grain from hotter climates where enzyme activity, broadly speaking, is lower. (There is more about whole-wheat flour in the next formula of 100% whole-wheat.)

▶ We often encourage students to experiment when it comes to the kind of whole-wheat they use. If you use a slightly higher protein white roller-milled flour, this can help prop up lower protein flours, such as einkorn, emmer, spelt, or Øland flour. This balances out the overall gluten levels, compensating for the lower levels of protein found in these whole-wheat flours. It means that the loaf will still be beautifully robust, and rise well during baking; this "propping-up technique" is one we often use to achieve higher sprung loaves while still using local or heritage whole-wheat flour.

We teach three versions of our classic formula. This is the second version. It is halfway between the School's classic sourdough loaf, which is just 20% whole-wheat flour, and the 100% whole-wheat version. It is made using 50% whole-wheat and 50% white flour, and the result is lighter than whole-wheat, while still offering much of the whole-wheat flavor and nutritional benefits. This formula needs slightly more water because it is whole-wheat, and the bran takes up more of the water.

You will notice subtle differences between this dough and the classic 20% sourdough, even with just a relatively small percentage change in the ratio of whole-wheat flour to white. It will ferment slightly faster, the crumb will be moister, and the sour flavor will be more pronounced.

Classic: whole-wheat sourdough boules

A good whole-wheat sourdough loaf has a robust crust and a tender crumb. Made with 100% whole-wheat, sourdough can be a more challenging loaf to bake, and many students who have attempted whole-wheat loaves before they attend the School express frustration that their bread hasn't turned out the way it should. But whole-wheat is worth persevering with, not least because it has buckets of flavor and nutrition. Baking a consistently good whole-wheat sourdough is easier to achieve when you understand why there are pronounced differences between flours. The two main considerations are the levels of bran and enzymes. Both affect your bread.

HOW THE MILLING PROCESS AFFECTS THE FLOUR

▶ The way in which flour is milled and sifted affects the quantity and texture of the bran. Large particles of fiber can interrupt the gluten network of your dough, and so compromise the structure of the crumb. There may also be marked differences in the openness of the crumb between stone-ground whole-wheat bread and one made with roller-milled whole-wheat flour. In general, the finer the whole-wheat flour is milled, the less the bran interrupts the gluten network.

▶ Stone-ground flour is also digested more slowly. Studies on sourdough made with stone-ground flour have indicated that the rate of assimilation for carbohydrates is slower than any other bread, making this a great loaf for anyone who needs to monitor or slow down blood sugar levels, such as athletes or diabetics (see page 199 for more info on blood sugar).

HOW ENZYMES AFFECT THE RATE OF FERMENTATION

▶ Using whole-wheat flour really tests the baker, because the fermentation of the dough is far more responsive when all the enzymes and nutrients are available to the microbes. I often compare it to driving a Formula 1 car when you have just passed your driving test—the dough can run away with you. Different whole-wheat flours are also milled using different grains that grow in different climates, and are then milled using different techniques. This becomes more relevant when you know that different grains also have varying levels of naturally occurring enzymes, which are affected by the humidity of the country or region in which they are harvested.

▶ Northern European countries have climates with higher humidity levels, so generally produce grains with higher levels of enzymes. When this grain is milled, the sugars are broken down faster, with the result that dough made with this kind of flour ferments faster. As more sugars are available to the lactic acid bacteria, they produce more acid, which results in higher levels of acidity in the dough, especially if left for too long. It is especially important when using European whole-wheat flour, to keep a close eye on the timings, as the dough can easily over-ferment. When this happens, the acidity compromises the gluten network, giving you a sour-tasting loaf.

▶ The lower humidity levels of parts of Canada and the USA, for example, results in a very dry harvest, and has the opposite effect on grain grown there. When there are very few enzymes in the grain, there is limited availability of sugars for the yeast to use, which slows fermentation. Sourdough made with low-enzyme flour ends up underproofed, pale, and as heavy as a brick, because the microbes don't get enough food, and the sugars are very quickly used up.

WHY DO DIFFERENT FLOURS BEHAVE DIFFERENTLY?

▶ Large mills auto-adjust their bread flour, so it is a matter of simply finding flour you like, and getting to know it. If possible, I recommend that home bakers make contact with their local artisan mill. If you can, visit the mill, find out more about the flour, and ask the miller about the Hagberg number—a measurement that indicates the levels of enzyme activity in the flour. Ironically the higher the Hagberg number, the lower the enzyme alpha-amylase, which can be hard to get your head around. Typical Hagberg numbers in the UK and northern Europe might vary from 200 to 400, while it tends to be higher in the US.

▶ Hagberg numbers on a dry summer harvest or from countries with a continental climate, can end up with a Hagberg number over 400, which makes flour low in enzymes. For this kind of flour, the mills have to adjust the enzyme levels or add malt; however in other countries, the rules vary and adjustments are not allowed.

PROTEIN LEVELS ARE DIFFERENT

▶ The amount of protein in flour is directly proportional to the amount of sunshine the plant gets, and so there are slightly lower protein levels in flour grown in temperate Europe. What we lack in quality of protein, though, we seem more than able to make up for in flavor, with more sugar being available. This is of course a generalization, but I think that it is a reasonable one to make, so you may need to get to know the optimal level of hydration, so as with all the formulas, the water may need slight adjustment according to the levels of protein of the flour you choose to use. In the end it is about getting to know your flour. Familiarity with your flour makes it easier to understand the small nuances of the baking process, which will make you a better baker.

Classic: whole-wheat sourdough boules

❯ INGREDIENTS

225g leaven (see pages 90–93)
900g water
1kg strong whole-wheat flour
24g fine sea salt

❯ INCLUSIONS

20g olive oil

❯ **SUGGESTED STARTER** Any, but for maximum sourness and digestibility, use rye or whole-wheat.

❯ **SUGGESTED METHOD** Retarded. This gives time for the bacteria to produce organic acids, which contribute to both flavor and digestibility.

Advice

▶ One of the things that can really help result in a stronger dough when making whole-wheat bread, is to extend the Mix & Autolyze step without the leaven. It gives time for the bran to soak up the water, and softens it, which in turn does less damage to the gluten network as you mix. An hour or so will make a real difference.

▶ I suggest that this is a loaf that is best refrigerated for 18–24 hours, however, for those looking for maximum digestibility, you can refrigerate this for an additional 12 hours—your loaf will have higher acidity and slightly less "oven spring."

▶ Stone-ground whole-wheat can sometimes be tricky to judge. When you first mix the dough, it looks as though there is not enough water, but after half an hour or so, the flour will have had a chance to absorb the extra water. You will need to be patient, and get to know your flour. Because whole-wheat flour is full of nutrients and enzymes, with plenty of food available to the microbes, it ferments more quickly than white flour, so you will need to reduce the bulk fermentation, and perhaps shorten the final proof. You need to become familiar with your flour, and get used to the rate at which it ferments, which means practicing and using the loaf record sheet (see page 75) to assess your dough, and make any changes to the schedule if needed.

▶ While all of the loaves in this book have been hand mixed, if you want full gluten development, I suggest that you mix this dough in the mixer. (See page 94 for further advice.) If you can get a spiral mixer, then even better, because the movement develops the gluten more than a planetary mixer (which is what most domestic mixers are).

▶ You will notice I added a touch more sea salt here—this will help develop the gluten. It's just a few grams, but it does make a difference.

▶ A small amount of olive oil in the dough will allow a fraction more extensibility of the gluten.

100% heritage sourdough in a pan

› INGREDIENTS

225g leaven (see pages 90–93)
   Again, if you suspect you can tolerate heritage grain, but not
   modern varieties, then use heritage flour to make your leaven.
875g water for the dough
1kg stone-ground whole-wheat "heritage grain" flour,
   such as einkorn, emmer, spelt, kamut®, or durum
20g fine sea salt

› INCLUSIONS

200g seeds such as pumpkin, sesame, linseed, or sunflower seeds
OR
200g sprouted heritage grain such as spelt, einkorn, or emmer
   (see page 48 for sprouting instructions)

› SUGGESTED STARTER Rye or whole-wheat

› SUGGESTED METHOD Retarded (and if you have digestive
issues, an extended retarded proof of 24–36 hours).
I also recommend a 12 hour pure autolyze in the fridge.

Advice

▶ Pre-soaking the seeds aids digestibility. Toasting the
seeds is optional—this increases the flavor, and stops
enzyme activity.
▶ Use butter to grease the pan, and dust with flour to stop
this loaf from sticking to the pan.
▶ I've suggested 875g water, but depending on the water
content of your seeds, you can use more. With dry-toasted
seeds, you increase this to 1000g of water.

If I suspect a student has digestive issues relating
to modern wheat (see page 186 for more on this),
I suggest they try a long, slow-fermented heritage
grain made in a pan, as many students report
that they find heritage grains easier to digest.
That said, don't be put off baking this loaf on
the grounds that you don't have digestion issues,
because the deep, nutty, sweet, complex flavors
are an absolute knockout.

There are several reasons for using a pan.
Firstly, heritage grains often have a more
complex gluten structure than modern wheat
varieties, and as a result, these ancient flours
can be challenging, especially for a beginner,
to make into a boule. Secondly, heritage grains
grown in a maritime climate have more enzymes.
Their activity massively boosts the amount of
sugars made available from the whole-wheat
flour, and so increases the amount of acid the
bacteria produce. Being coupled with a long,
slow, cold proof, and a rye starter, pushes the
acidity levels as high as possible, which break
down the gluten matrix, so the pan helps to
support the loaf as it proofs. It is not essential to
ferment this loaf using a long, slow proof, but if
you like a really sour loaf, or you have digestive
issues, this is the key component in reducing
the pH levels, and so potentially making this
bread more easily digestible.

There is no need to stretch and fold this loaf
more than once—just mix the *bassinage* water
in thoroughly. Also omit scoring.

Russian rye bread

❯ INGREDIENTS

750g leaven (see pages 90–93) or leftover discard from your starter
750g water for the dough at 170°F
1kg whole-wheat rye
24g fine sea salt

❯ INCLUSIONS

10g charcoal powder, optional
3 tablespoons lightly toasted coriander OR caraway seeds
50g molasses

❯ **SUGGESTED STARTER** Rye
❯ **SUGGESTED METHOD** Ambient or retarded

Advice

❱ Instead of making a leaven, use 700g of starter that is between 1 day and 1 week old, made up of accumulated starter discard. If older than this, it can become too sour to use. We keep the leftover starter in a separate pot in the fridge ready to make this bread.

❱ Occasionally, depending on the flour you use, the dough may need a little more water. If this is the case, first mix what you have, and then add just 10g more at a time, giving the dough time to absorb it. I have used some rye flours that can take up to another 200–250g.

❱ This is a very thick, sticky dough. I advise using a dough hook on a sturdy stand mixer to mix.

❱ There are two significant adjustments to the timings and schedule: Firstly, the initial autolyze is WITHOUT leaven for 4 hours. Maintain the dough temperature at 82°F. Another tip is to remove the leaven from the fridge when you scald the flour to allow it to come up to room temperature.

❱ Add the salt and any inclusions at the same time as the leaven.

❱ Once the leaven is added, the bulk ferment temperature should be allowed to drop to 72–75 °F— this is just a matter of leaving the dough aside at room temperature.

❱ To further intensify the flavors, you can smoke this bread by using a tablespoon or two of coriander seeds. See page 52 for smoking method.

This dark, moist, treacly bread has a distinctively Russian character, and is best left for two days before eating to really develop the flavors. We serve it toasted, topped with thick slices of beet-cured salmon and sour cream, sprinkled with dill.

The method used to make it differs from the classic method of sourdough in several ways and is actually much simpler:

❱ The leaven is made up of leftover sourdough starter, so there is no need to make leaven.

❱ There is no need to stretch and fold the dough, because rye flour lacks gluten to develop, and the technique relies on gelatinization.

❱ The shaping involves literally just squashing the dough together, and putting it in a well-floured banneton. You just need to use a generous dusting of flour to stop your hands from sticking to the dough.

❱ The flour is scalded using hot water.

WHY SCALD THE FLOUR?

Amylase enzymes naturally present in the dough peak at 170°F, so scalding milled whole-wheat rye, which is rich in natural amylase, kills off any naturally present yeast and bacteria. This creates a sweeter bread, because the amylases are not killed, so as the dough cools, they are free to convert the starches to simple sugars. When 3–5 hours later, the leaven is added, there is more sugar available. This increases the contrast of sweet and sour flavor, and is very typical of Russian-style rye breads.

Seeded sourdough boules

› INGREDIENTS

225g leaven (see pages 90–93)
850g water for the dough
700g white bread flour
300g stone-ground whole-wheat flour
20g fine sea salt

› INCLUSIONS

300–400g seeds, EITHER toasted lightly OR pre-soaked overnight
200g selection of seeds to roll the dough in, two-thirds of which
   will be returned to the pot

› **SUGGESTED STARTER** Any, but for maximum sourness and
digestibility, use rye or whole-wheat.

› **SUGGESTED METHOD** Retarded. This gives time for the bacteria
to produce organic acids, which contributes toward the breakdown and
digestibility of both the seeds and bread.

Advice

▸ You can use dry seeds, but when soaked overnight and
drained thoroughly, they are even more moist and delicious.
At the School, we also like to toast seeds lightly to give a
lovely nutty flavor.
▸ Soaking the seeds overnight certainly seems to increase
ease of digestibility, and adds to the open texture in the
dough. This is recommended for the ambient method.
Dry seeds tend to soak up some of the water, effectively
reducing the available water to the dough, and can result
in a tighter crumb structure. To compensate for this, you
can add another 20g of water. I recommend this for the
retarded method.
▸ It is best to add the seeds in during the stretch and fold
process; that way there is minimal interruption to the
gluten network.

When it comes to seeds, the sky is the limit. They
provide the chance to layer more texture, flavor,
and nutritional value into your loaf, for next
to no effort. You can either add them into the
dough, or simply roll your dough in them as you
do the final shape.

We have a huge collection at the School: golden
linseeds, flaxseeds, dark green pumpkin seeds,
sunflower seeds, fragrant sesame seeds, chia
seeds, and amaranth seeds, to name just a few.
Certain seeds combine well with particular
flours. Sunflower seeds and spelt, for instance,
have a natural affinity. it is worth noting that this
is the same technique used to add malted flakes

HOW TO ADD SEEDS TO
THE OUTSIDE OF YOUR LOAF

If you want seeds on the outside of your bread,
you will need about 200g to get decent coverage,
though the dough won't take up all of them. The
best way to do it is to put the seeds onto a wet
dish towel that has been wrung, to dampen the
outside, then scatter them on a shallow-lipped
plate. Just before you transfer the dough into
the banneton, very gently roll the dough in the
seeds. As you transfer the dough to the banneton,
close the dough as if you were closing a book, to
increase the tension and distribute the seeds. You
can, of course, scatter some seeds into the bottom
of the banneton, but this technique distributes
them more easily. Sift and return any remaining
seeds to a pot. There is usually about two-thirds
left to use next time.

Blackberry, poppy seed, & pea flower water bread

› INGREDIENTS

225g leaven (see pages 90–93)
800g butterfly pea tea for the dough (see below)
850g white bread flour
100g whole-wheat flour
50g rye flour
20g fine sea salt

› INCLUSIONS

200g blackberries or black currants
100g poppy seeds
20g toasted anise seeds, optional
Honey soy glaze (see facing page), optional

› SUGGESTED STARTER Any, however rye will give a great base flavor, and deepen the color.

› SUGGESTED METHOD This is one to try using each of the different starters, and each of the different methods, to see the variation between the loaf colors. Using a retarded method with rye leaven, accentuates the flavor of the berries in this bread, and deepens the color, but using a white starter and an ambient method, will give you a lighter colored and flavored loaf.

› MAKE THE BUTTERFLY PEA TEA Brew 2–3 heaping tablespoons of butterfly pea flowers in 800g hot water just off the boil, in the same way as you might make a pot of tea. Leave to cool, strain, and then warm to the temperature needed to create your ideal dough fermentation temperature.

The appearance of food and the desire to eat it are indisputably connected, and this loaf is a real showstopper. The dramatic blue crumb is achieved by using butterfly pea flower tea in place of water. The tea is made from a Southeast Asian flower which turns the dough an amazing color without affecting the flavor. When the ambient method is used, you will get a midnight-cobalt blue crumb, but if you develop the acidity of the dough more using the retarded method, it transforms the bread into a rich violet color.

It is an amazing way to demonstrate that the length of fermentation and the resulting changes in pH affects more than just the taste in the loaf. It's as though the loaf is a giant litmus paper; as the pH increases, the colors deepen to purple.

We grow our own blackberries and black currants in the School gardens, and the deep blues and purples set off the berries and poppy seeds beautifully. The option to include toasted anise seeds and a honey soy glaze, means that you can match the flavors to the intensity of the color if you want to.

Advice

▶ The more butterfly pea flowers used in the tea, the darker the loaf.

▶ White roller-milled flour best shows off the color, though sometimes lacks the complexity of flavor I like in my bread, so if you want to layer in more flavor, add 20g of toasted anise seeds to the dough, and mist the loaf with a honey and soy glaze.

▶ HONEY-SOY GLAZE Mix 2 tablespoons of dark soy sauce and 2 tablespoons of honey with 2 tablespoons of water. This quantity will mist four loaves, and stores in the fridge for a month. Mist the loaf lightly using a reusable spray bottle 2–3 minutes before the bread finishes baking.

Ramson boules

> INGREDIENTS

225g leaven (see pages 90–93)
775g water for the dough
800g white bread flour
200g whole-wheat flour
20g fine sea salt

> INCLUSIONS

For the herb butter
A large handful of ramson (wild garlic) leaves, plus extra to decorate
100g ghee or unsalted butter
A large handful of grated hard cheese, such as Parmesan
Coarse sea salt and ground black pepper, to season

Chop the ramson directly into a mortar in the tiniest lengths possible using scissors, then add the butter and mix thoroughly. Stir in the cheese. It should be thick enough to spread easily. Season with salt and pepper. To store, cover and keep in the fridge for up to a week.

> SUGGESTED STARTER Any

> SUGGESTED METHOD Ambient or retarded

In April, the garden at the School comes alive. The birds sing their hearts out, and the cherry trees are laden with blossom. The ramson, with its pretty, star-shaped flowers, is tucked under an ancient beech tree at the bottom. Making a herb butter with it is a wonderfully easy way to get a rich, full-flavored sourdough bread. I love to use a mortar and pestle rather than a blender, simply for the joy of it: I cannot deny myself the satisfaction of crushing the ingredients together. The butter is added to the center of the dough on its final shaping, and trickles and oozes through the bread as it bakes.

Advice

▶ Ramson (wild garlic) is only in season for a couple of months of the year, so if you can't find any, or when it is out of season, use oregano, marjoram, coriander, parsley, sage, or a herb of your choice. Or use lemon or orange zest and cinnamon at Christmas.
▶ Be absolutely certain that what you are using is ramson—it looks remarkably similar to poisonous plants such as lily of the valley. It should smell like garlic, but if in any doubt, do not use.
▶ Don't be tempted to overload the boule with paste, and make sure all the butter is inside the boule. Don't overdo the shaping or it will burst out of the sides.
▶ Line the banneton with ramson leaves and any flowers for a very pretty effect.

ADDING THE HERB BUTTER TO THE DOUGH

Open the dough flat, and put a good tablespoon or two of the butter on top. Spread out, leaving 2 inches around the edges without butter.

Fold down each edge so that all the butter is inside.

Shape by first stretching the dough from the bottom up. Then pull the sides of the lower half together, followed by the sides of the upper half, and then pull the top down before rolling it down. Create tension in the dough by drawing it gently back against the table top and then drop in the banneton.

Turn the dough over.

Place the reserved leaves in the banneton.

Dust the banneton well.

Stitch if you can see any butter by pulling the dough together to seal the butter in.

Jalapeño & cheese loaf

› INGREDIENTS

225g leaven (see pages 90–93)
20g olive oil
800g water
700g white bread flour
200g sifted whole-wheat flour
100g cornmeal (maize)
10g malt powder (see page 51)
18g fine sea salt

› INCLUSIONS

6 jalapeño peppers preserved in oil, chopped
200g strong cheese such as Cheddar, grated

› **SUGGESTED STARTER** Any

› **SUGGESTED METHOD** Ambient—I love a sweet,
milky-flavored loaf that allows the cheese and heat
to take center stage.

Often we think of bread as an addition to a meal, but with inclusions, it can also be the centerpiece. This Mexican-inspired loaf was made by one of our students, Phil, and was so good that it had to be included. There is real joy in seeing our students go on to create their own amazing breads.

The jalapeño peppers are added at the last stretch and fold. In general, they are mild, but packed full of flavor. Occasionally, though, you get a rogue one that is super hot, which is part of the fun of eating them, I guess!

Advice

▶ Cornmeal can come in many different grades, from fine to coarse and stone-ground or roller-milled. This will affect the texture and the amount of water it will soak up, so it is worth trying a few to see which one you prefer.

Olive and pickled lemon butter bread

> INGREDIENTS

225g leaven (see pages 90–93)—a rye leaven will
  give you a sourer flavor
800g water
800g white bread flour
200g whole-wheat flour
15g fine sea salt

> INCLUSIONS

200g pitted olives
100g cultured butter
3 pickled lemons, very finely chopped, rind only
8–10g pink peppercorns, crushed
4 juniper berries, finely chopped

> **SUGGESTED STARTER** White or rye

> **SUGGESTED METHOD** Ambient, using a white starter for a fresh
sweet loaf, or retarded with a rye leaven for increased sour tang.

Advice

The salt in the bread has been reduced slightly as both
the olives and the lemons are salty. Only use the rind
when chopping the lemons, as the lemons themselves are
too acidic, and can affect the gluten structure.

These robust, tangy ingredients make for an
intense, yet harmonious flavor combination, and
a loaf that really lends itself to being the center
of a Mediterranean feast. I love it with soft goat
cheese, Prosciutto, and a bottle of fresh crisp
white wine.

LAYERING IN FERMENTED INGREDIENTS

Like sourdough, pickled lemons and olives are both
fermented, and like any good partnership, they
bring out the best in each other, emphasizing the
sourness, salty brininess, and aromatic flavors.
The original inspiration came to me while churning
our cultured pickled lemon butter that we serve
for lunch. The bread can take more flavor than the
butter can, so I've used the same ingredients,
but added more of the pickled lemon. Juniper
berries bring complex, but subtle aromas, as do
the pink peppercorns, which I love, as they are so
exquisitely fragrant.

This bread is perfect for learning how to control
flavors. When deciding how sour you want it to be,
you need to choose between starters and leaven.
Our original, homofermentative, French starter,
which is lactic and sweet, makes a young, fresh
loaf when fermented ambiently that highlights the
lemony flavors. When I want to emphasize the
sourness of the loaf, I use a rye starter, and add
about 50g grated Parmesan to the butter, which
adds a rich umami flavor. I proof this slowly for
24 hours using the retarded method. Both versions
are good, and part of the fun of developing your
understanding of sourdough, is playing with flavor
development, and discovering what you like.

Tomato & herb bread

› INGREDIENTS

225g leaven (see pages 90–93)
800g water for the dough
700g white bread flour
300g durum wheat semolina
20g fine sea salt

› INCLUSIONS

For the tomato and herb paste
200g sun-dried tomatoes, chopped
50g tomato paste
3 garlic cloves, chopped and lightly sautéed
6 1-inch stems of fresh oregano
   or 2 heaping tablespoons of dried herbs
1 tablespoon ground black pepper
50g finely grated Parmesan

Pat the sun-dried tomatoes lightly with kitchen paper to remove the oil. Add the tomato paste, sun-dried tomatoes, garlic, oregano, and Parmesan to the dough by smearing the bread with the paste, and scattering the rest of the inclusions on top of this at the final shaping stage.

› SUGGESTED STARTER Any

› SUGGESTED METHOD Any

Not everyone likes adding things to their bread, but it's worth trying this out. It doesn't take much to transform a humble loaf of bread into the centerpiece of a meal. The addition of the durum wheat semolina to this loaf adds a gorgeous texture reminiscent of *Altamura* bread from Bari in southeast Italy, and I am unapologetic in my greediness when it comes to this loaf. It's the sort of bread to pull apart with your hands, and eat at a table laden with cheese and wine. I love to breathe in its sweetness, but I can't stop there. The aroma is so good, that I will wipe chunks of it across my plate, saturating each one in the vinaigrette from a summer salad, enjoying every mouthful.

This formula uses sun-dried tomatoes, their intense flavor matching that of the oregano. We grow several kinds of oregano at the School, and in summer it fills the air with its perfume, which has a natural affinity with tomatoes. The tomato paste and herbs are added at the last possible moment, so that the acidity of the tomato paste, and the natural antifungal properties of oregano do not inhibit dough development.

Advice
▶ Check that your tomato paste is not too acidic. There is not a measure for this, so you will have to rely on your sense of taste to find a sweet one.
▶ Use a tablespoon of the semolina scattered on the baking surface as you turn out the dough, to create a bit more texture.
▶ Durum wheat semolina adds texture and flavor, but it can suck up a lot of the water. If you find this to be the case, increase the water incrementally up to 870g.

Scandinavian buttermilk sourdough

> **INGREDIENTS**

225g leaven (see pages 90–93)
850g buttermilk for the dough
500g white bread flour
500g heritage whole-wheat such as einkorn,
    emmer, or Øland flour
20g fine sea salt

> **INCLUSIONS**

20g lightly toasted caraway seeds

> **SUGGESTED STARTER** Rye or whole-wheat, or chocolate.

> **SUGGESTED METHOD** Any method

Advice

Commercially made buttermilk doesn't have the same
richness that my buttermilk brings to this formula,
so if you buy your buttermilk, you will need to add about
20g of butter to it.

A Nordic-inspired loaf, this is made using 50% whole-wheat flour, which I mill literally seconds before adding it to the dough. It also combines toasted caraway seeds and lightly acidic cultured buttermilk, which I make myself; often this has a few missed bits of butter in it, which adds extra richness to the bread and softens the crumb.

I first came accross Øland, a Scandinavian heritage wheat flour, in a bread baked by Rasmus Kristensen at Noma in Copenhagen. The flavor of the sweet, moist, and rugged bread he made stayed with me, as did the restaurant's approach to serving it. Diners were given just a small slice, as they knew this would mean the customers would take the time to savor it, almost as though it were a fine wine. I love this idea of taking the time to appreciate something humble. So often bread is put on the table and taken completely for granted. It is a thought that has stayed with me ever since; savor your bread, slow down, breathe deeply, and just lose yourself in the delicate, complex, wheaten, malted, honeyed, sour and sweetness.

Despite the fact that I play with flavor and layer aromas by using various flours and ingredients throughout my baking, in the end it is the addition of whole-wheat and the long slow fermentation that I find are the keys to getting the best flavor.

Sweet berry bread with rose water
served with crushed fermented berries

❯ **INGREDIENTS**

225g leaven (see pages 90–93)

whisk together for the dough:
120g water
400g milk
2 large eggs
125g melted butter

650g white bread flour
350g whole-wheat flour
20g fine sea salt

❯ **INCLUSIONS**

300g fruit such as strawberries or blueberries, lightly crushed
30g rose water (optional) for misting (see recipe below)

❯ **SUGGESTED STARTER** White

❯ **SUGGESTED METHOD** Either ambient or retarded are fine

Advice

▶ Add the salt at the same time as the liquid.
▶ There is no need to stretch and fold.
▶ This bread only needs one shape even when using the retarded method.
▶ Reduce the oven temperature with this bake to 375°F. This needs to be more cake-like, so remove from the oven when lightly golden about 10 minutes earlier than the master method timings. If you want a soft crust, wrap it in a clean dish towel as it cools.

This bread, which has more of a cake consistency, is an enriched, sweeter sourdough made with butter and eggs. I often talk about layering fermentation and flavors, so we serve it with crushed fermented strawberries (from early summer, parts of the garden are covered in wild strawberries), tart cultured cream, and *kvass* made with summer fruit. It is best when lightly sour, so I recommend using the ambient method to get the most lactic flavor possible.

Serve with sour cream and fermented berries. Simply mix together about 300g of berries and cover in a live ferment, such as water kefir or fruit vinegar, with a small amount of sugar and leave overnight. Drain well, crush with a fork and sprinkle with superfine sugar.

❯ **FERMENTED ROSE WATER**
In the summer we make fermented rose water at the school, with which we mist this loaf just as it comes out of the oven.
10–15 red or pink rose heads,
  unsprayed
1 cardamon pod, crushed
400g water
100g sugar

Separate the petals and rinse lightly. Place in a saucepan with just enough water to cover (no more, or you'll dilute the intensity of their flavor). Cover and simmer for 10–15 minutes, or until the petals have lost their color. Strain and discard the petals. Return the liquid to the pan and reduce it by just over half so you have about 200g of liquid. Stir in the sugar. Cool and transfer to a sterile glass jar with a lid. It will keep for about 6 months in the refrigerator.

Advice

▶ If you prefer a sweeter version of this loaf, substitute the hazelnuts with 200g of soaked and drained golden raisins.

▶ Adding golden raisins can increase the sugar in the chocolate porridge, which can significantly increase the rate of fermentation, even though it is added at the last moment, in the last stretch and fold. Keep an eye on the dough, as you may need to shorten the bulk fermentation to compensate.

Chocolate & roast hazelnut bread

❯ INGREDIENTS

225g leaven (see pages 90–93)
830g water for the dough
800g white bread flour
200g whole-wheat flour
80g cacao
15g roasted barley malt (see page 51)
20g fine sea salt

❯ PORRIDGE

100g dark chocolate, 80% cocoa solids, melted
70g rolled oats
230g water (or more if needed)
200g chopped toasted hazelnuts OR
300g golden raisins, soaked in warm water overnight and drained well

❯ **SUGGESTED STARTER** Chocolate or white (French)

❯ **SUGGESTED METHOD** Any, though the ambient method encourages a more lactic, sweeter-flavored loaf.

❯ **A SEASONAL TWIST** At Christmas, you could combine the grated zest of an orange, 2 tablespoons of whiskey, and a tablespoon of honey mixed with 2 tablespoons of water. Bring it to a boil, then strain and transfer to a spray bottle. About 2 minutes before the end of baking, use this to mist the loaf, then return to the oven. This gives the loaf a beautiful shine. It is not so much a flavor, as an aromatic suggestion on the outside of the crust.

Chocolate and roast hazelnuts are a classic combination, but we also make a sweet version of this bread with plump, juicy, golden raisins.

Many people don't realize that flavor of chocolate is dictated, to a certain extent, by the fermentation process. There is a natural synergy between fermented foods, and I like to use a chocolate starter for this bread, which is likely to contain microbes that were involved in the breakdown of the cacao, as it adds complexity and bittersweet cacao notes. Studies show that a range of homofermentative lactic acid bacteria is involved in the breakdown of cacao, as the temperature of cacao fermentation is very warm. This starter should therefore give you a lovely milky-flavored bread.

The sourness is perhaps lost until the loaf is a few days old, but it rarely lasts that long! I sometimes grate in a little nutmeg on the last stretch and fold, largely because I associate chocolate with the Caribbean, and in particular with the island of Grenada, which is where we source the chocolate we use at the School. It's a good combination.

We serve this bread with sweet cultured butter whipped with confectioners' sugar and cacao (to taste).

Rosinbrød

> ## INGREDIENTS

225g leaven (see pages 90–93)
825g water for the dough
600g white bread flour
300g whole-wheat flour
100g rye flour
20g fine sea salt

> ## INCLUSION

BUTTER SPICE PASTE
85g unsalted ghee, or very soft butter
60g soft brown sugar
1 teaspoon vanilla extract
2 teaspoons ground cinnamon
½ teaspoon freshly grated nutmeg
400g golden raisins

Mix the butter, sugar and spices, then stir in the golden raisins.

> ## SUGGESTED STARTER Rye or whole-wheat

> ## SUGGESTED METHOD Either ambient or retarded is fine

This Scandinavian-inspired loaf has all the elements you would expect in a traditional rosinbrød—or raisin bread. It is dark, sweet, rich, and fragrant, with a small amount of rye, and a buttery spice paste that oozes and trickles through the center of the dough as it bakes—the aroma from the oven is unbelievably good. It's excellent when it is a few days old, in large, lightly toasted hunks spread with cold butter, and served with a pot of tea.

We tend to use ghee instead of butter to make the paste, as it has a higher smoke point. If you use butter, it can burn if any escapes as the bread bakes.

Advice

❱ There is extra sugar in this bread from the paste and the raisins, so you will need to keep an eye on the bake time—check it 10 minutes early and remove from the oven if it has reached a light golden tan color.

❱ Although there is a high level of hydration, the golden raisins soak up a good deal of the water, as do the whole-wheat and rye flours, so this bread has a moist, slightly denser crumb structure. Choose moist, plump golden raisins, as they will require less water to hydrate them.

❱ Make sure your paste is smooth and easy to spread. Smear over the dough at the point where it is at its most open as it is shaped.

❱ See Ramson Boules (page 133) for step-by-step instructions for adding the butter spice paste.

Beets, black pepper & feta cheese batards

› INGREDIENTS

225g leaven (see pages 90–93)
100g water
750g beet purée for the dough (see recipe below)
800g white bread flour
200g rye flour
20g fine sea salt

› INCLUSIONS

400g feta cheese cheese, chopped into 1-inch cubes
1 teaspoon cracked black pepper

› SUGGESTED STARTER Any, but for maximum depth of color, sourness, and digestibility, use rye or whole-wheat.

› SUGGESTED METHOD Retarded, again for depth of color. This method gives time for the bacteria to produce organic acids, which contribute to the deep purple color and to flavor and digestibility.

› BEET PURÉE
4 large beets, washed and dried
1 tablespoon olive oil
Rub the beets with olive oil, then wrap them in a piece of aluminum foil, place on a baking sheet and roast at 425°F for 1 hour or until soft. Remove from the oven and allow to cool. Keep the skins on. Liquidize in a blender, adding a little cold water if needed, until you have a purée about the same thickness as applesauce. Use to make the dough when it reaches 82–86°F.

When I began playing with beets, I wasn't convinced it brought anything other than a red color and an earthy flavor. My opinion changed when I threw in a little tangy feta cheese, and a good pinch of fragrant black pepper. These bring out the gentle sweetness of the beets, pushing any traces of earthiness into the background, so it becomes a partner in a wonderfully creamy, salty, and peppery mix. When fermented slowly using the retarded method, the increased acidity levels of the dough help to preserve the color in the bread. This is especially pronounced when using a (heterofermentative) rye starter because it encourages the production of acetic acid. A very long, slow proof—24 hours in the fridge—also increases the intensity of the color.

Advice

▶ Beets aren't to everybody's taste. If you are a gardener, and want to grow your own for this formula, botanist James Wong recommends the variety "Detroit Dark Red" because it has a less earthy flavor.
▶ Pumpkin will produce similar results, and give a wonderful orange color. You might need to adjust the thickness of the purée—it should be pourable.
▶ You can add thin slices of beets just as you shape the dough, which will result in deep purple flecks of color in the crumb.
▶ Shaping a batard is almost exactly the same as making a boule. Once you've formed your boule, rest it for a minute to allow the gluten to relax, then dust the top with a small amount of flour and put your hands into the middle of the bread. Rock gently back and forth, keeping the seam underneath to form two fat cylindrical shapes with tapered ends. Proof either on a *couche* (a linen fabric specially made for breadmaking) or a heavy-duty cotton dish towel.

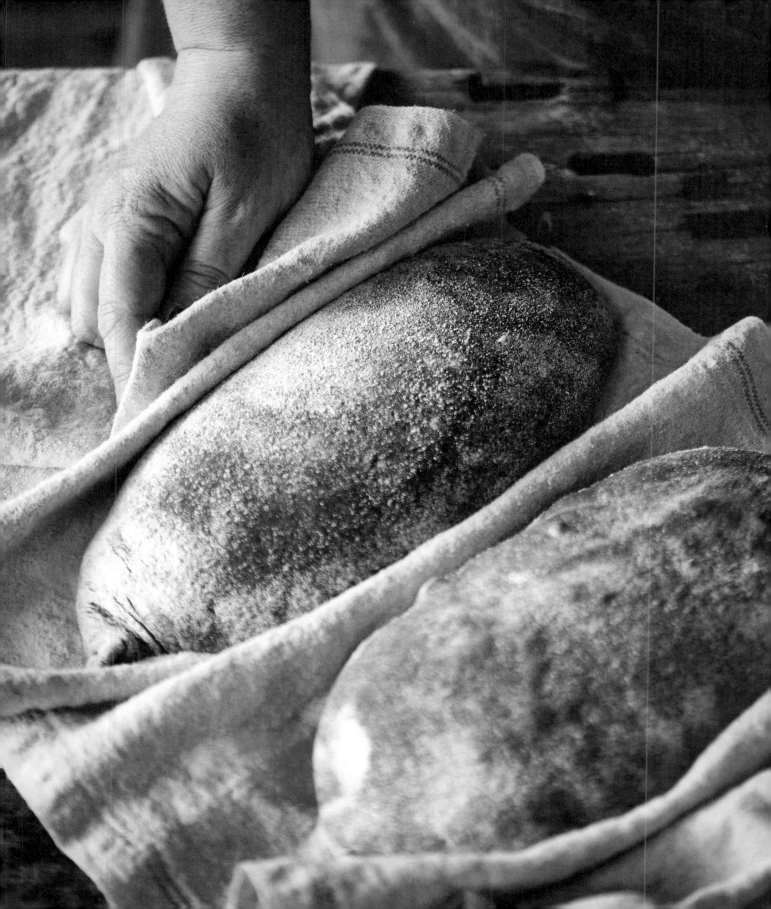

Earl Grey, fig, & kamut® loaf

› **SCHEDULE**

225g leaven (see pages 90–93)
800g Earl Grey tea
500g kamut® flour (whole-wheat)
500g white bread flour
20g fine sea salt

› **INCLUSIONS**

6–8 fresh figs OR 150g dried figs, soaked overnight and drained
Finely grated zest of 1 large organic unwaxed lemon,
 to be added on the last stretch and fold
30g organic polenta or cornmeal, for dusting

› **SUGGESTED STARTER** White

› **SUGGESTED METHOD** Either ambient or retarded

Khorasan is an ancient wheat that originates from the Fertile Crescent that includes Afghanistan and Iran. The grains, which have a beautiful distinctive amber color and a slightly glassy appearance, are double the size of most wheat, and produce a wonderful, buttery, textured yellow flour. They are also characteristically hump-shaped, and so have the nickname "camel's tooth." Khorasan is known by the commercial name kamut®.

It grows strikingly tall, with golden ears and long, black, whiskery awns. I've grown some in my garden, and while the plant is perhaps slightly compromised by the lack of sunshine, it is, nevertheless, well worth saving a few grains and planting them in a sunny spot just for the joy of seeing how beautiful it is.

The bergamot in the Earl Grey tea and lemon are gorgeously aromatic, and echo the eastern flavors of the flour. Khorasan can be a very thirsty flour, so some flours need another 50g of water.

Advice

▶ Depending on the time of year, use either fresh or dried figs. If you use dried figs, the soaked fruit can become very hydrated, so you might need to reduce the tea by 20g. Conversely, if you use fresh figs, you may need to adjust the hydration by adding an extra 20–30g. It is often a question of trial and error when using fruit in sourdough, so remember to keep a loaf record, and adjust your liquid accordingly the next time you bake.
▶ When you shape, keep the fruit inside the loaf as much as possible, as if it is on the crust, it is likely to burn.

Smoked kibbled rye & wild cherry sourdough

› INGREDIENTS

225g leaven (see pages 90–93)
850g water for the dough
800g white flour
100g rye flour
100g whole-wheat flour
20g fine sea salt

› INCLUSIONS

200g kibbled smoked rye grains
200g dried sour cherries, pre-soaked and drained
100g sprouted rye, optional

› SUGGESTED STARTER Any

› SUGGESTED METHOD Retarded

Advice

▶ Occasionally we add sprouted rye for extra chewiness and texture. See Sprouting (page 48).
▶ See Smoking (page 52).
▶ There are various ways to obtain fruitwood. The most obvious is to simply forage or find a tree, and to ask the owner if you can swap wood for bread. Alternatively, carpenters and local artisan woodworkers will often save you wood shavings, or consult the list of resources on page 202.
▶ The enzymes and pentosans (sugars) in the rye provide a boost to fermentation in both the leaven and the dough, by making more sugars available to the yeast, so it is a good idea to reduce the bulk fermentation for the ambient method by about 30 minutes or so.
▶ This loaf has a darker, more caramelized crust, but do check its progress at the end of baking.
▶ If you smoke your loaf, do so lightly. Less is more! The gorgeous flavors that develop from smoking sourdough are all about subtle suggestions around the crust, rather than a loaf that tastes like it has been in a bonfire.
▶ You can kibble your own grains in a mortar and pestle or mill, if you struggle to find any.

This loaf is all about flavor that matches texture. The freshly smoked, kibbled grains bring a chewy texture, and impart a fruity sweetness, reminiscent of German rye breads. Paired with the rich and fruity tones from the cherrywood smoke, they take on an extra dimension, resulting in a beautifully complex loaf. In late summer we dry fresh Morello cherries, which I like to soak, and then mix into the dough to add an irresistible sweet–sour tang.

Of course you don't have to stick to using rye grains, there are many other possible combinations, each with their own appeal. Think spelt and apple wood, or emmer and maple. I love to sprout and smoke the naked oats that heritage grain grower John Letts sometimes drops in to me, using sweet mulberry wood cut from the tree outside the School. If you like something with a bit more smokiness to it, lightly smoke your loaf after you bake it. If you add sprouted rye, then reduce bulk fermentation to 3½ hours as the rye is pretty active.

Miso & sesame

❯ **INGREDIENTS**

225g leaven (see pages 90–93)
800g water for the dough
700g white bread flour
300g strong whole-wheat flour (lightly sifted which produces
  a lighter loaf)
5g fine sea salt
50g miso paste

FOR THE ROUX
100g white flour
325g water
30g sesame seed oil
Mix the oil and water in a pan over low heat. Stir continuously, adding the flour a little at a time until it forms a thick paste. Cook for an additional 3–5 minutes, stirring continuously. Allow to cool. Add to the dough at the end of mixing.

❯ **INCLUSIONS**
100g lightly toasted black sesame seeds AND 100g lightly toasted white sesame seeds (for rolling the dough in)

❯ **SUGGESTED STARTER** Any

❯ **SUGGESTED METHOD** Any

Close your eyes and hold on to this moment. Taste the saltiness and depth of the miso, smell the aroma of toasted sesame, feel the crust crunch and the yield of the softest sweet aromatic crumb.

Is there a formula to love? Perhaps not, but this gets pretty close. We make and ferment our own *koji* and miso, so it seemed natural to layer in the fermentation, and use miso in our bread.

This formula includes toasted sesame seeds and fermented soybean miso, and uses techniques borrowed from the Asian Tangzhong bread method, which softens the crumb beautifully. This method involves making a roux using flour and water, which is mixed and heated to 149°F in much the same way as porridge. This gelatinizes the flour and forms a translucent pudding-like paste. As the bread bakes, starch granules in the dough absorb water and swell up. The starch in the roux is already swollen to its maximum, so incorporating the roux into the dough means the starch does not have to compete with the proteins to absorb water as it bakes, and so it makes a softer, more hydrated crumb.

Advice

▶ Use a good-quality unpasteurized miso for the best flavor.
▶ Keep in mind that the process of cooking the flour to make a roux denatures the gluten. The gluten in the rest of the flour in the formula is needed to provide the gluten network. The small amount of oil adds more intensity to the flavor, but also tenderizes the crumb and allows lightly increased extensibility.
▶ The miso and salt are added together. The amount of salt is reduced, to balance the high level of salt in the miso. You may not even need any salt, depending on the levels of salt in your miso—adjust to your taste accordingly.

Soy, ginger, & rice sourdough boules

› INGREDIENTS

225g leaven (see pages 90–93)
750g total water
100g soy sauce (this has roughly 20g salt)
200g strong whole-wheat flour
800g white bread flour

› INCLUSIONS

400g cooked sushi rice.
  Cook the rice, leave to cool, and use at 79–82°F.
  Mix in just before the first fold.
100g chopped stem ginger, drained of its syrup
20g sesame oil
10–20g seaweed, such as dulse or nori,
  soaked in water for 2 hours, drained, and chopped finely
40g *koji* rice, for rolling the dough in

› SUGGESTED STARTER White

› SUGGESTED METHOD Ambient or retarded, though the ambient method will make a sweeter-tasting bread.

This loaf, which is perfect with thin slices of smoked salmon, was inspired by my love of sushi. The inclusion of sushi rice adds a lovely chewy gelatinous characteristic to the dough.

I often compare flavor to a chord played on the piano: top, middle and bottom notes combined. This sourdough is harmonious, especially when made with our white, French sourdough starter. When this starter was analyzed by microbiologist Marco Gobbetti at the University of Bari in Italy, he and his team identified bacteria *kimchi*, a facultatively heterofermentative microbe, as one of the dominant strains. This particular microbe produces more lactic acid, which means that the dough ferments with a more delicate base flavor, allowing the notes of sweet ginger, sesame, and soy to take center stage, and explains why it produces a milkier, lighter-flavored bread.

Advice

▶ Check the salt content of the soy sauce. Look for one with 16g salt per 100g of sauce.
▶ Keep an eye on the speed of fermentation, as the temperature of the water in this formula is higher than usual.
▶ At the School, we ferment our own *koji* and use it to roll the dough in just before it goes into the banneton, in the same way as you might roll the dough in seeds or malted flakes. *Koji* is available from specialist Japanese shops, but a handful of ordinary rice, slightly overcooked and patted dry, would have a very similar effect if you can't find it.

Pumpkin & polenta sourdough

❯ INGREDIENTS

LEAVEN follow the master method, using the ingredients below
30g white French starter
300g cooked, drained, mashed pumpkin
100g white bread flour
30g water at 95°F

750g water for the dough
  mixed with 100g cooked pumpkin
800g white bread flour
200g whole-wheat flour, sifted
20g fine sea salt

❯ PORRIDGE INCLUSIONS TO BE FOLDED IN

400g cooked polenta
200g pumpkin seeds, soaked overnight and drained well
100g golden raisins
20g pumpkin pie spice—to dust lightly over the water
  added to the dough in the last bassinage.
200g pumpkin seeds, for rolling the dough in

❯ **SUGGESTED STARTER** White—it is soft and allows the pumpkin to come through.

❯ **SUGGESTED METHOD** This is best made using the ambient method. However, if you want to use the retarded, swap the white flour in the pumpkin leaven for sifted whole-wheat.

Sweet, aromatic and tender, with a soft crumb and burnt orange crust, this is a loaf that can take center stage on a chilly autumn evening; the kind that calls for a wooden table, a large bowl of steaming soup, and a roaring log fire.

Once I've stopped dreaming about eating it, I have to turn to the practical side of making this bread. This is an advanced bread, because it uses a porridge, and the technique to make the leaven is new. When vegetables such as sweet potato, or in this instance, pumpkin, are added to the leaven in the form of a purée, you get a more controlled rise, as the natural sugars have already been consumed by the microorganisms in the leaven. This is particularly important for this loaf, because I've added golden raisins for extra sweetness.

I also use the pumpkin and cinnamon sourdough powder (see page 46) to dust the top of the loaves when I score them, which is a great way to get contrasting flavor and color.

Advice

❱ As polenta cooks, it bubbles like a volcanic spring. Take care not to get burned. Keep the stovetop heat moderate, and stir constantly with a wooden spoon. The longer you cook your polenta, the firmer it becomes.
❱ The small amount of spice powder is lightly dusted over the dough just as the water is added in the final *bassinage*. Adding the spices in a small quantity at the last stage, insures they don't retard the fermentation, or overpower the bread. It is a hint, not a hit of spice.
❱ Be sure to choose plump golden raisins. Older, dried ones will take water away from the dough.

Honeyed porridge loaves

› INGREDIENTS

225g leaven (see pages 90–93)
840g water for the dough
200g strong stone-ground whole-wheat flour
800g white bread flour
10g non-diastatic malt powder if using a roller-milled white flour
  (see page 51)
22g sea salt

› INCLUSIONS

**400g PORRIDGE Cook the porridge, then set aside to cool to 82°F.
Mix in by smoothing it in during the stretch and fold (see page 99).**

320–340g water
  Different oats take up varying
  amounts of water, so some
  discretion is needed here.
80g rolled oats
60g lightly toasted wheat germ
40g honey
200g barley flakes to roll the
  dough in

› SUGGESTED STARTER Any, but rye really brings out the flavors.
› SUGGESTED METHOD Any

Advice

▶ A higher protein flour will give this dough structure as porridge has no gluten.
▶ Mix well when adding the water to the flour, and do full stretch and folds to develop the gluten.
▶ Lightly toasting wheat germ brings out the flavors; 5 minutes in a warm oven (325 °F) is usually enough.
▶ Barley malt extract is a delicious alternative to the honey.
▶ Adding an additional 100g of water in 20g increments will give the loaf a more open crumb, but this is best done only if you are an experienced baker. The extra water can increase enzyme activity, so will also speed the fermentation up.
▶ For an extra shine and sweetness, dissolve a tablespoon of honey in 2 tablespoons warm water, pour into a spray bottle, and mist the loaf 3 minutes before the end of baking.

Creamy oats, toasted wheat germ and honey are classic ingredients that belong together. This is my perfect loaf, the one I dream of, but it is one that requires a real understanding of the dough and the process. The key to the voluptuous, open, honeyed crumb in this loaf is in the higher hydration, the addition of the porridge, and the timings. I could wax lyrical about how good this loaf is; it really is the most delicious, sweetest sourdough. But flavor-wise, as much as this combination is a match made in heaven, it is also about the synergy between the amazing taste, and just how good oats are for us (see page 34).

I wish I could claim that I discovered the way to get such a gorgeous gelatinized crumb, but I can't take the credit. This method is one that was created and shared with me by possibly one of the most instinctive and brilliant sourdough bakers in the world, Richard Hart. While head baker at Tartine Bakery in California, he developed a technique of adding in the porridge during the stretch and fold, after a conversation with an old original hippie one afternoon while standing in the queue in a bakery in Sonoma Valley in California. The genius is in the timing of adding the porridge to the dough as it is stretched and folded, which significantly increases the gelatinization of the crumb.

Yogurt light spelt boules

> INGREDIENTS

225g leaven (see pages 90–93)
800g liquid for the dough
    160g whole milk yogurt mixed with 640g water
500g finely milled whole-wheat spelt flour
500g finely milled white spelt flour
22g fine sea salt

> INCLUSIONS

15g fennel or caraway seeds in the bottom of the banneton.

HONEY WATER To make a honey water with which to mist the loaf, add 2 tablespoons of dark honey to 30g of hot water, stir well, and transfer to a spray bottle. Remove the loaf from the oven about 2 minutes before the end of baking, mist, and return to the oven.

> **SUGGESTED STARTER** Chocolate

> **SUGGESTED METHOD** Ambient

This loaf is sweet, milky, and light, with a sour tang and a hint of fennel in the crust.

Modern spelt is the closest we have to the earliest forms of bread wheat. In evolutionary terms, spelt is the great-niece of einkorn and the daughter of emmer, and represents a turning point: before spelt, flours from the ancient grains produced much less extensible dough. Making bread with spelt flour can be challenging. Spelt generally has lower levels of proteins that are balanced in a way that means you have to work hard to get the gluten to its optimal point. It is dough that benefits from having two or three extra stretch and folds and a good deal of mixing as you add the flour and water. Salt strengthens the gluten too, so I have used slightly more in this formula.

Advice

▶ The soft flavors of spelt lend themselves to honey and yogurt. The yogurt will soften the crumb. Adding honey can speed up fermentation, so you might want to reduce the bulk fermentation slightly. Do remember to keep a record of your timings and temperature, and adjust your next bake accordingly.
▶ Many students who visit the School report that they find spelt easier to digest. It's almost impossible to say exactly why this is, but for a discussion on this see page 186. A very good tip if you do suspect that you have digestive issues with undigested flour, is to use sourdough powder (see page 45) to dust, or potato flour for the bannetons as using ordinary flour means that there will be remnants of undigested flour on the outside of the loaf after it has been baked.

Kefir milk sourdough loaf

› INGREDIENTS

750g fresh milk kefir for the dough
    fermented for no longer than
    12 hours overnight OR buy some from a store
20g melted butter
650g white bread flour
350g whole-wheat flour
20g fine sea salt
225g leaven (see pages 90–93)

› INCLUSIONS

1 teaspoon freshly grated nutmeg
    to dust the banneton

› SUGGESTED STARTER At the School, we use the white French homofermentative sourdough starter, as it further enhances the production of lactic acid, keeping the light, milky tone of this bread.

› SUGGESTED METHOD Any

Using a milk product in sourdough is one of the easiest ways to soften the crust and the crumb. We serve milk kefir in the mornings at the School, and I often get asked whether it can be used on its own to make sourdough, but to be honest, I don't recommend it. On occasion, I have made superbly fermented sourdough using just kefir milk, but getting the kefir to be at its peak can be challenging, especially for those new to fermenting. The yeasts in milk kefir can also be less active than those in a starter, so although the loaf's crumb may be full of flavor, it may not have much rise.

So this version uses both kefir milk and starter to get the best possible rise and flavor, as well as a small amount of butter, which really accentuates the flavor.

As it bakes, this rich, buttery loaf produces aromas reminiscent of bread pudding.

Advice

▶ I use a teaspoon of freshly grated nutmeg in the flour as I shape—perhaps because the smell of baked milk reminds me of rice pudding—just for the flavor in the crust, rather than a full-on taste in the loaf.
▶ The leaven (which is effectively a microbial war zone for food) has lots of competing microbes, so can become over-acidic quite quickly. A good tip is to make sure that you use the leaven as soon as it is ready.
▶ For bakers who want a soft crust, wrap your bread in a clean cotton dish towel while still warm, for about an hour, and then remove. This moistens the crust.

Malted muesli boule

> INGREDIENTS

225g leaven (see pages 90–93)
750g water for the dough
500g malted flour
500g white bread flour
20g sea salt

> INCLUSIONS

First cook the muesli in the same way as you would oatmeal and allow to cool
120g dried muesli porridge
200–250g water
  You may need to adjust the water to muesli ratio
  as different brands will take varying amounts of water.

200g malted barley flakes to roll the loaves in

> **SUGGESTED STARTER** Any, though rye will give a great base flavor.

> **SUGGESTED METHOD** Retarded for maximum digestibility.

This loaf has a voluptuous, chewy, creamy crumb, and the malt brings both amazing sweetness and a rich, deep, burnished color to the crust. The flavors remind me of a bowl of warm porridge served with cream and whisky I was once treated to in Scotland.

The muesli creates the creamy texture, and complements the flavors and textures of the flaked malted oats, wheat, and seeds, as well as the malt in the flour. It's a great loaf to enjoy at breakfast with marmalade. The benefit of this formula is that the diversity of grains provides a diverse range of food for your gut microbes, and so can help contribute to your gut health (see page 188 for more on this).

We make our own muesli, but if you are buying your mix, look for one that's organic with no added sugar, and packed with nuts, seeds, and malted flakes. Some varieties of muesli will need more water than others to make the right consistency of porridge, so the amount of water advised is approximate.

Advice

▶ As this dough contains both malt and porridge, it can be challenging for beginners. Running your hands under very cold water, and drying them before you shape, can make handling the dough more manageable.

▶ The important thing to understand here is that the simple sugars made available to the microbes, accelerate the rate of fermentation, so you will need to shorten the timings to accommodate this, or you will end up with a sticky mess, especially if the weather is warm. I can't give exact timings for shortening the process, as this depends on the ambient temperature of your kitchen, but, as a rough guide, at the School we cut about an hour off the autolyze when using the ambient method, and about 30 minutes off the bulk fermentation when using the retarded method.

Einkorn & spent ale grain sourdough

› INGREDIENTS

225g leaven (see pages 90–93)
835g water for the dough
700g white bread flour
300g einkorn whole-wheat flour
20g fine sea salt

› INCLUSIONS

200g golden raisins
200g spent beer malted grains (see advice below)

› SUGGESTED STARTER Any

› SUGGESTED METHOD Any

Advice

▶ I'll admit that spent grain is not an ingredient that is easily available. It involves finding someone who runs an artisan brewery, and having a conversation with them to see if they might be willing to give you some spent grain in exchange for a loaf of bread. It's not your typical trip to the supermarket, or even a click online, but neither is this your typical loaf. It's about being creative and connecting to the world. It's worth getting more spent grain than you need as it freezes well.

▶ If you can't find a brewer, you can substitute with grain flakes, which have been soaked in beer for an hour and drained. If you use malted grain, you will need to shorten the bulk fermentation using the ambient method by about 40 minutes.
▶ Finally, and perhaps most importantly, become familiar with how the dough feels as you mix, fold, and shape. Learning to instinctively trust your senses and slow down and feel, separates the good bakers from the truly amazing ones.

This is a loaf that celebrates the origins of bread. Beer and bread have been bound together for so long, that the origins of their connection are forgotten, but we know from inscriptions on the walls of Egyptian tombs, that they were fermented side by side thousand of years ago, and although it is rare that they meet as ingredients, they nevertheless belong together.

This technique uses 30% einkorn, a rich dark, nutty, aromatic heritage grain that is the first grain known to be cultivated. It has low extensibility, so in order to get a good boule shape, and take advantage of its gorgeous flavor, we blend it with a modern variety. Perhaps as an extension to this history, we decided to use this as part of the blend of flour that we make our spent grain bread with.

When I teach, I often talk about connecting to your dough, and this formula is one I always encourage people to mix by hand. There is joy in both connecting with the ingredients and other artisan makers; when you mix grains, water, flour, and wild yeast, you should appreciate what goes into the dough. Making a good craft beer, like making bread, is about using your senses, so take the time to find and talk to your local artisan brewer.

Cracked black barley & stout bread

> INGREDIENTS

225g leaven (see pages 90–93)
800g water
200g strong whole-wheat flour
800g white bread flour
20g roasted barley malt powder (see page 51)
20g sea salt

> INCLUSIONS

PORRIDGE MADE WITH CRACKED BLACK BARLEY
100g black barley
350g stout beer
100g barley popcorn (see below)
**Cook the porridge slowly, adding in the stout a bit at a time. It should be thick enough to coat the back of a spoon, and not too runny. If it cooks too quickly, you will need to add more water to compensate for evaporation, so add 4 teaspoons water at a time, and keep cooking until it
is gelatinous. To make the barley popcorn, soak the whole barley overnight in water, drain well and dry, then toast lightly until it pops. Add the popcorn to the cooked porridge, then set aside to cool and use at 82°F. Fold in on the last fold for a marbled effect.**

200g wheat flakes to roll the dough in

> **SUGGESTED STARTER** Any, however rye
will give a great base flavor to this loaf.

> **SUGGESTED METHOD** Retarded for
maximum digestibility.

This is a fantastically chewy, richly textured loaf, with a complex aroma that is almost like licorice. Black barley is a small, gorgeously glossy dark grain. It is used in beer production to make malt, as it has coffee and chocolate flavors that are reminiscent of stout. Using stout as the liquid therefore echoes the flavor of the barley.

I'm the first to admit that this is not a beginner's loaf. It's a challenge, but it's fun to play, and once you get into the routine of making sourdough, you will want to experiment with new textures and flavors. When we first tried using black barley, we began by milling it into the flour and also tried using sprouted grains. In the end, we settled on milling the barley on an open setting on one of our small flour mills to make cracked black barley, and then used this to make "porridge" with the beer. If you don't have a mill, grinding the grains using a mortar and pestle is almost as effective. Making the barley into porridge is what made a real difference to the texture and flavor of the bread. For an additional burst of flavor, we also toast some of the barley to add a sweet popcorn taste to the porridge—the grains split, then pop when you toast them, and they smell amazing.

Black barley is, for the most part, unchanged from when it was first cultivated (unlike pearl barley, which has been hulled, steamed, and polished) and so is sometimes referred to as a heritage grain.

Advice

▶ Black barley isn't always easy to get hold of, but specialist beer suppliers sometimes stock it. We simply googled it and bought it online. If you can't find any, some supermarkets now sell ready-cooked black and pearl barley, which is a great substitute— simply use this instead of making a porridge and substitute water for stout for a very similar loaf.

▶ The higher alcohol levels in the stout will negatively affect the fermentation, so using the beer to make the porridge removes the alcohol and helps to hydrate the barley. Barley can be a very thirsty grain, and the amount of stout needed can vary— the porridge should be the same thickness as the consistency you make for breakfast.

Sourdough baguettes hybrid & 100% sourdough

> INGREDIENTS

For the 100% sourdough version
225g leaven (see pages 90–93)

For the hybrid
225g leaven
5g organic fresh yeast mixed with 20g water

770g water for the dough
900g white bread flour
100g strong whole-wheat flour
10g non-diastatic malt powder (see page 51)
20g toasted wheat germ (optional)
20g fine sea salt

> SUGGESTED STARTER White (homofermentative)
for a sweeter, lighter, traditional French flavor

> SUGGESTED METHOD Retarded

Baguettes might seem simple, but in fact they are one of the most challenging sourdoughs to make, requiring both practice and a degree of skill. That said, once you have mastered making them, they are so good, you will probably never buy a commercially-produced baguette ever again.

A good baguette is an integral part of French culture. The ones I grew up eating in southwest France were made in the traditional way with only a tiny amount of yeast (about 1%) combined with a sourdough starter that was kept very lactic, (see page 61), which produced a light, open crumb, a very gentle tang, and a wonderfully chewy crust. The long, slow fermentation associated with sourdough is one of the reasons that French baguettes always taste so amazing.

When planning the breads to be included in this book, I was of two minds about this technique of combining commercially-produced yeast with sourdough. Some sourdough purists will be throwing their hands up in horror, but I felt it was important for people to understand that yeast can, when used in combination with a sourdough starter, produce a slightly different flavor, and potentially, a more open crumb. Also that it is not the yeast itself that is the key to the magic, but the symbiotic relationship with the lactic acid bacteria, which alters the pH of the bread. It is this dual fermentation, and the production of organic acids by the lactic acid bacteria, that is the key to the changes in flavor and digestibility of the bread. So, if you are a purist, and want to do this without yeast, simply follow the master method. If you want to try the combined method, please use organic yeast, which has far more synergy with our ethics at the School.

Advice

▶ In France, baguettes are usually about 20 inches long, but for a domestic baker, the best advice I can give is to measure both your oven and your baking stone, and to use these as your guide.

▶ Steam is essential to get a good spring in the oven. At the School, we use a spray bottle to add a fine mist as the breads go into the oven. Another way to add steam is to put a large baking pan into the bottom of the oven and allow it to preheat. As the loaves go into the oven, pour a large cup of water into the bottom of the pan, which creates plenty of steam.

▶ For either method extend the autolyze WITHOUT leaven or yeast for 2–4 hours. This allows for maximum gluten development.

▶ For the hybrid version, reduce the dough temperature to 73–75°F.

▶ The retarded method needs just 30 minutes bulk fermentation with only one stretch and fold. It is then shaped AFTER the overnight ferment in the fridge. So cover the bowl with a damp cloth, put it in the fridge, and shape the following morning. Effectively this means that the dough has a longer final proof at ambient temperature once it has been shaped.

▶ One of the reasons this is a demanding bread to bake, is because the skill lies as much in the timing of the fermentation as in the handling of the dough, so shape gently, but firmly. This takes practice, and you will get better at it over time.

▶ Bake time is reduced to 20 minutes.

▶ Whenever possible, we use French T65 flour for the baguettes, but if you can't get it, a fine ground white bread flour, or a lightly sifted stone-ground whole-wheat flour will work. You might need to shop around and compare the texture of a few flours.

▶ The wheat germ is optional, and has been added mainly to intensify the aromatic toasted flavor.

Advice for the hybrid version

▶ The timings for the hybrid version are slightly shorter because the commercial yeast proofs the dough faster.

▶ For the ambient method, reduce the time of the bulk fermentation to 2 hours.

▶ For the retarded method, just 30 minutes bulk fermentation should be enough, then refrigerate overnight in a cooler part of the fridge at 41°F, and give a final proof of just 1½ hours.

BAGUETTE SHAPING

There are as many shaping techniques for baguettes as there are days in the week, and different hands like different techniques, so it's worth watching our online video.

If, like me, you get overwhelmed with trying to get the perfect baguette (I nicknamed this challenge "baguetettegate"), relax and remember that the purpose is to create tension while maintaining the air—a bit like putting a seal on the tire of an old-fashioned bike—to insure the baguettes hold their shape, and are firm enough to score.

Baguettes are easier to shape when the dough is ever so slightly underproofed.

Begin by turning out the dough onto the table, and dividing it into four 500g pieces. Use plenty of flour on your hands, but not too much on the work surface.

Take the first piece and fold one edge into the center of the dough, then fold the other side to join in the middle. Press down along the join with your fingers to create a seal. Be gentle, but firm, and try not to knock the air out.

Using your thumb, roll the dough over itself to create tension, but take care not to deflate the dough. Stretching it in this way will create tension that insures stability.

Roll the dough back toward you, then roll away from your body with pressure on each side to taper the ends.

After this first roll, stop and let the dough relax. Leave it for a minute or two before shaping again.

Time & sequence guide for 100% sourdough baguettes

These are the timings for the 100% sourdough we make at the School. Please read them through before you begin baking. To accommodate your flour and ambient temperatures, you may need to adjust these timings.

STEP	AMBIENT	RETARDED
REFRESH STARTER For a white starter or chocolate starter	**Day 1: 11 A.M.** But if you are going to work then 8 A.M. would be ok	**Day 1: 11 P.M.** Leave out on the side overnight
OR for a whole-wheat or rye starter	**Day 1: 5 P.M.**	**Day 1: 6 P.M.** Leave out on the side until 10 P.M., then refrigerate overnight
MAKE LEAVEN	**Day 1: 11 P.M.** (see page 91)	**Day 2: 8 A.M.** (see page 93)
MIX & AUTOLYZE without leaven	**Day 2: 6 A.M.**	**Day 2: 8 A.M.**
CONTINUE WITH AUTOLYZE & MIX IN LEAVEN	**Day 2: 8:30 A.M.**	**Day 2: 12:30 P.M.**
ADD EXTRA WATER & SALT	**Day 2: 11 A.M.**	**Day 2: 1–1:15 P.M.**
BULK & STRETCH & FOLD	**Day 2: Until 1 P.M.**	**Day 2: 3 P.M.** once the bulk fermentation has finished, you need to cover the dough with a damp cloth, and leave overnight in the fridge
SHAPE	**Day 2: 1–2 P.M.**	**Day 3: 8 A.M.**
FLOOR TIME		
FINAL PROOF	**Day 2: 2–4 P.M.** You can put it in the fridge for half an hour to firm up	If your fridge is 41°F or below, leave the dough for another hour on final proof
BAKE	**Day 2: 4:30–6 P.M.**	**Day 3: 10–10:30 A.M.**

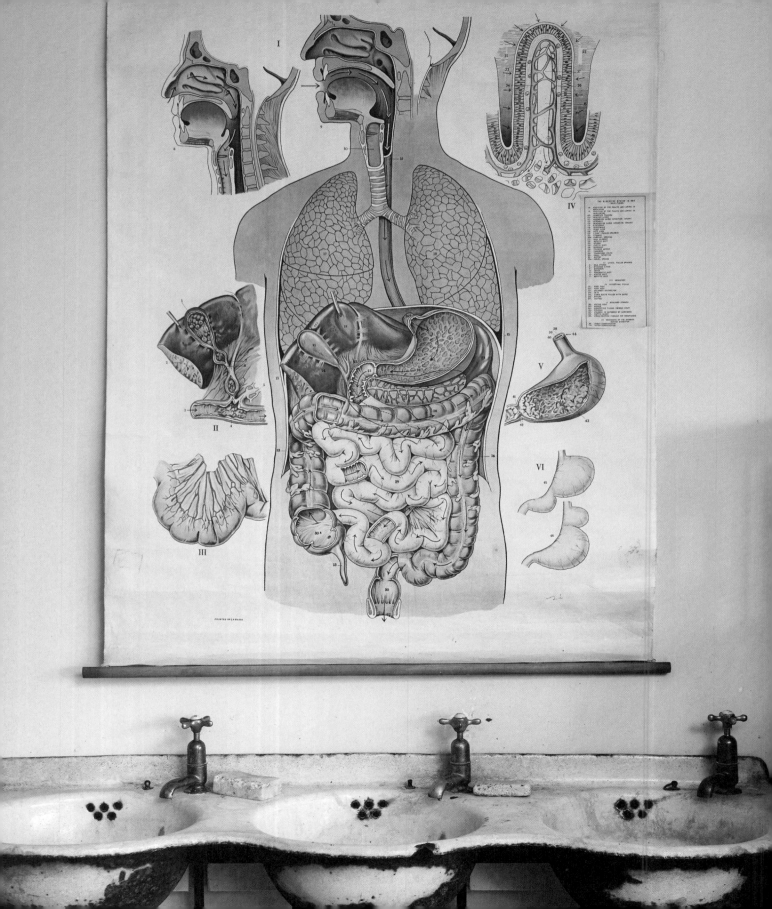

Digestibility
& nutrition

The more I researched into the history of bread, the more obvious it became that my digestion problems were part of a much wider picture. Not only is sourdough easier to digest, it is more filling, nutritious, and delicious than industrially produced bread—but why?

The madness of modern bread

Bread has been part of our history since Neolithic times. Its development covers every aspect of life, from when survival depended on the harvests, all the way to recent industrial advances. Today, there has never been a more exciting time to bake, as the revival of ancient milling techniques, modern microbiology, and sourdough fermentation collide, allowing us both to understand and bake the most delicious and nutritious bread possible: sourdough.

Records show that until the Industrial Revolution, almost all bread was fermented long and slow using wild yeast, lactic acid bacteria, and stone-ground flour. Then, almost overnight, everything changed as technological advances in the agricultural, manufacturing, and baking industries happened simultaneously.

In the early twentieth century, millers altered their process from stone-ground to roller-milled, industrialized yeast manufacturers abandoned lactic acid bacteria, and botanists got busy narrowing the genetic diversity of wheat. Modern breadmaking uses fast-acting yeast and rolled milled flour. The entire process takes about 1½ hours. Without lactic acid bacteria, none of the component parts of the flour are broken down. The magic is in the fermentation, and the acids that are produced are key to predigesting the break, making it more nutritious, nourishing, and easier on people with digestive malaise.

The processed bread on our supermarket shelves is completely dependent on petrochemical-derived, synthetically fertilized, and adulterated wheat, routinely treated using carcinogenic, chemically produced herbicides. The wheat used to make the bread is stripped of its nutritional properties; it is fast-processed using a single monoculture yeast strain; the bread is packed with preservatives, emulsifiers, and enzymes before being packaged in wasteful plastic bags, and transported long distances. It is bread that is destroying our health and our planet.

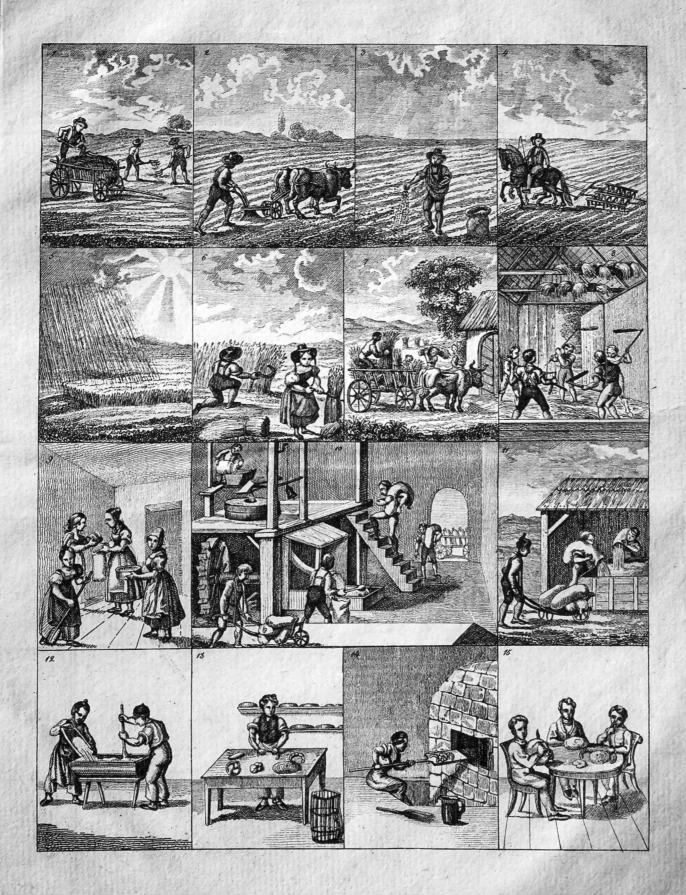

The health benefits of sourdough

It's a complicated picture, so the best place to start is with an overview of reactions to wheat.

(IgE) An allergic reaction to wheat involves IgE (immunoglobulin) antibodies reacting to wheat proteins. It results in the production of histamine, and is a fairly fast reaction by the body, sometimes causing swelling, wheezing, asthma, including wheat-dependent exercise-induced asthma, and contact urticaria (hives), which is an immediate, localized, but transient swelling and redness on the skin after direct contact with wheat or flour. It represents 11–25% of diagnosed food allergies.

AUTOIMMUNOGENIC (IgA/IgG) These are generally slower reactions and include auto-immune diseases such as celiac disease, which affects 1% of the population, and is triggered by gliadin, one of the proteins that makes up gluten. Other reactions include dermatitis herpetiformis (similar to eczema) and gluten ataxia, with symptoms such as abdominal pain, double vision, constipation, and diarrhea.

NON-CELIAC GLUTEN SENSITIVITY Estimated to affect about 6% of the population, this is where eating gluten leads to symptoms that improve once it is removed from the diet. These symptoms include headaches, joint and muscle pain, a foggy mind, nausea, abdominal pain, diarrhea, and constipation. Unlike wheat allergy and celiac disease, gluten sensitivity does not have a recognized set of symptoms. Doctors cannot tell if someone is suffering from it by examination (although there is a blood test, it doesn't give accurate results for many patients). So this sensitivity can only be diagnosed by ruling out other diseases and then trying a gluten-free diet.

There is another factor to consider here too, which is that although gliadin might be the trigger for celiac disease, and be the protein at the heart of many reactions to wheat, it is not the only protein in grain that can cause sensitivities; it could be albumin, globulin, gliadin, glutenin, or gluten, and just to make things even more confusing, there are also many sensitivities to wheat that are neither non-allergic nor non-autoimmune. One of the most common of these is irritable bowel syndrome and there are reports of up to 20% of the population suffering from IBS.

Many people with issues digesting fast-fermented bread report that they have a problem with gluten, but often they are self-diagnosing and wrongly blaming gluten. In many cases people suffering from IBS may be sensitive to fiber, fermentable oligosaccharides, disaccharides, monosaccharides, and polyols (FODMAPS), and phytic acid. There is more on how long, slow fermentation helps to stop IBS symptoms later in this chapter.

Sourdough is not gluten-free—that is a term covered by legislation. In the US, only foods that contain 20 parts per million (ppm) or less can be labeled gluten-free. However, in a study on gluten degradation headed up by renowned sourdough microbiologist Marco Gobbetti at the University of Bari in Italy, the residual concentration of gluten in 48-hour fermented sourdough was 12ppm and albumins, globulins, and gliadins were completely broken down.

Professor Gobbetti's study, published in 2004, first provided me with concrete evidence that sourdough was breaking down gluten. The study indicated that long, slow fermentation modified the parts of gliadin and glutenin in wheat flour that are toxic to individuals with celiac disease. I've subsequently had the opportunity to discuss these findings with Professor Gobbetti. He explained that people were never able to fully digest gluten without the aid of long, slow fermentation, because our digestive systems are relatively fast. The very long, slow fermentation process of sourdough predigests the indigestible amino acids proline and glutamine in the gluten. Proline is resistant to breakdown by the enzymes in the bowel (also reported by celiac specialist Alessio Fasano), so the only way we can break it down, is through using *lactobacillus* and long, slow fermentation.

It is worth noting that this study looked at dough fermented for 48 hours—a much longer fermentation than normal. This suggests that the retarded method of making sourdough results in more digestible bread than faster methods of making sourdough. To take advantage of this, you can leave the sourdough in the fridge for 48 hours, but there will be roughly a 20% drop in the oven spring. However, this may be a price worth paying if you are after maximum gluten degradation.

I must stress that a laboratory-controlled experiment done under medical supervision does not offer people suffering from celiac disease or wheat or gluten allergies the green light to start eating sourdough bread. For obvious reasons, anyone with allergies should discuss this with their doctor first. There is also always the potential for sourdough to have cross contamination with undigested flour.

IS GLUTEN DEGRADATION IN SOURDOUGH THE ANSWER TO DIGESTING BREAD?

For many people it is. One of the main reasons that people with wheat sensitivity report that they find sourdough easier to digest is, I believe, down to the degradation of gluten during the long, slow fermentation. That said, the degradation of gluten actually depends on many factors, including the acidity of the dough, the length of fermentation, the kind of microbes in the starter, the kind of proteins, and the levels of them in the flour—it really is very individual.

THE
TRANSFORMATIVE
POWER OF
FERMENTATION.

The gut microbiome

I stopped being able to digest wheat after taking a large dose of antibiotics. One of the most frustrating aspects of this was not understanding why I couldn't eat bread. I was a baker, and not being able to digest wheat literally drove me away from my career. What on earth was I meant to do if I couldn't eat what I baked?

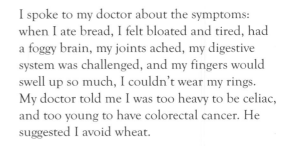

I spoke to my doctor about the symptoms: when I ate bread, I felt bloated and tired, had a foggy brain, my joints ached, my digestive system was challenged, and my fingers would swell up so much, I couldn't wear my rings. My doctor told me I was too heavy to be celiac, and too young to have colorectal cancer. He suggested I avoid wheat.

I also visited a specialist at a well-respected clinic in London. She was a traditionally trained doctor who specialized in herbal medicine. It turned out that I did have some food allergies, but she acknowledged that I also had multiple intolerances. She suspected I had intestinal permeability or hyperpermeability (leaky gut syndrome), explaining that my system had been severely compromised by many factors, including multiple antibiotics and steroids for asthma. She told me to avoid wheat completely, and for four years that's what I did.

It was during my conversation with this doctor that I first heard of the microbes in our digestive tract—the gut microbiome. Their job is to break down food into nutrients that our bodies can use. They also act like soldiers, providing a barrier system that protects the body from unwanted pathogens. The more diverse your microbial population, the more robust and healthier your digestion, which in turn supports your overall health.

WHY IT'S IMPORTANT TO HAVE A HEALTHY GUT

Over the past 20 years, more and more research has pointed to gut health being integral to our overall well-being. Gut bacteria are able to produce a variety of vitamins, to synthesize all essential and nonessential amino acids, and carry out biotransformation of bile. They provide the vital biochemical pathways for the metabolism of non-digestible carbohydrates,

which include large polysaccharides, such as resistant starches, cellulose, hemicellulose, pectins, and gums, and some oligosaccharides that escape digestion. Many intestinal bacteria produce antimicrobial compounds that compete for nutrients, and for site of attachment in the gut lining, thereby preventing colonization by pathogens. This is known as the barrier or competitive-exclusion effect. A robust healthy gut microbiome is vital to a healthy digestive system, and because the intestinal lining is the initial defence for our immune system.

The epithelial or outer layer of intestinal cells is connected by structures that firmly adhere adjacent epithelial cells to one another, forming a seal that prevents macronutrients, such as proteins, and other ions, escaping into our bloodstream without a screening process. If your gut microbiome becomes compromised, your intestinal lining can become porous or permeable, and there is a risk that your body treats the unexpected entry of such molecules as "invaders", and triggers your immune system to set off a response. Inflammation is a natural immune response, and causes even more stress to your system. As a result, each time you eat a food that contains the macronutrient that your body has registered as a threat (such as the proteins found in grains), it turns its attention to battle. Often the foods that you eat most (such as wheat) become the trigger for your immune response. It is exhausting, and over time can lead to your body fighting itself, and to an array of autoimmune diseases, including IBS, celiac disease, Crohn's and diabetes.

These microbes are with us almost from the moment we are born, to the moment we die, but to understand more, I went to leading health specialist and author of *The Diet Myth* Professor Tim Spector. Tim has a specific interest in gut microbes, triggered by the realization that genetically identical twins in some of his clinical studies had different health issues, and very different gut microbes. He explained that intestinal permeability or hyperpermeability is a small part of a complicated picture. What is perhaps more relevant, is that the diversity of microbes in those eating a Western diet is typically 30% lower than it was 50 years ago, which might also play a contributing factor in the obesity epidemic. Scientists are only just beginning to fully understand the role and complexity of the microbiome, as they are still identifying which bacteria are beneficial, and how to boost them. Tim is optimistic: "It's hoped that in future we may be able to manipulate gut bacteria to overcome illnesses, such as irritable bowel syndrome and even obesity." The best way to support the gut microbiome, he explained, is through including in the diet plenty of fiber, phenolic compounds (see page 192), and the widest variety of grains, and fruits and vegetables possible.

WHY SOURDOUGH IS GOOD FOR GUT HEALTH

One of the key things I learned as I read study after study, is that slow-fermented bread was the missing piece of the puzzle. The fermentation facilitates a remarkable change in the flour, which in turn transforms the bread, resulting not just in increased nutrients and nourishment for us, but for our microbes too. The creation of an abundance of the specific kinds of fiber, food, and nutrients means that sourdough is a prebiotic. Prebiotics feed your friendly bacteria, and help them proliferate on their own, nourishing and supporting the microbes that are absolutely key to our health—the same kind of microbes found in the soil, and in our starters. To me, this is proof absolute that sourdough is the link that connects us. It is microbial magic.

Fiber

Sourdough can increase your dietary fiber intake by a whopping 10–15% compared to yeasted bread. The ratio of soluble to insoluble fiber can also be manipulated, depending on how long you ferment your dough. Soluble fiber helps to slow the emptying process in our stomachs, which makes us feel fuller. It also helps to lower cholesterol and stabilize blood glucose levels. Insoluble fiber absorbs water to help to soften the contents of our bowels, and support regular bowel movements—it also helps to keep us full, and keep the bowel healthy.

There are two main groups of fiber, soluble and insoluble. Soluble fiber helps to slow the emptying process in our stomachs, which makes us feel fuller. It also helps to lower cholesterol and stabilize blood glucose levels. Insoluble fiber absorbs water to help to soften the contents of our bowels, and support regular bowel movements—it also helps to keep us full, and keep the bowel healthy. The ratio of soluble to insoluble fiber in your bread can be manipulated, depending on how long you ferment your dough.

Research by The Institute of Medicine has found that the average American adult eats only 15g of fibre per day, while the recommended amount is 25g for women and 38g for men—so bread takes on an even more important role as a potential source of fiber. Beneficial microbes feast on fermentable fibers found in whole grains. They resist digestion by our enzymes as they pass through the digestive tract. These fibers arrive in the large intestine relatively intact, where our microbes can extract the fiber's extra energy, nutrients, vitamins, and other compounds. Short-chain fatty acids obtained from fiber are of particular interest, as they have been linked to decreased inflammation, improved immune function, and protection against obesity.

The changes in the way we grow, mill, and ferment bread go some way toward explaining why the modern diet is exceedingly fiber-poor by historical standards.

Studies have shown that slow-fermented sourdough has 20–30% higher levels of a fiber called resistant starch compared to breads baked using just yeast. Resistant starch passes through the digestive tract unchanged—in other words, it is resistant to digestion, and functions in much the same way as soluble fiber.

There has been a great deal of research into resistant starch, but one of the most significant health benefits, is that it provides food for the friendly bacteria in the gut. As this is broken down by our gut microbes, they release short-chain fatty acids, which have also been shown to have a positive influence on gastrointestinal permeability. One of these short-chain fatty acids is called butyrate, which is an ideal fuel for the cells that line the colon. So resistant starch feeds both the friendly bacteria, and indirectly, the cells in the colon, by increasing the amount of butyrate. The short-chain fatty acids that are not used up by the cells in the colon travel to the bloodstream, liver, and to the rest of the body, where they may have various other beneficial effects, with research indicating they could well provide protection against diabetes, and may reduce the risk of developing gastrointestinal disorders, cancer, and cardiovascular disease.

People often comment about how full they feel after just one slice of sourdough, and there have certainly been some interesting studies on how resistant starch creates a feeling of satiety and can help contribute to weight loss, by increasing feelings of fullness, and reducing appetite. This increase in resistant starch helps explain one of the mechanisms by which the long, slow fermented bread eaten in the diabetes studies conducted by Professor Terry Graham slowed down blood sugar response. There are also some studies which have shown that resistant starch also reduces the pH level, which in turn has beneficial effects on the colon, including reducing inflammation, and reducing the risk of colorectal cancer (the fourth most common cause of cancer death worldwide). There are no human controlled trials yet, but I think it is fair to say that resistant starch could be considered therapeutic for various digestive disorders, including inflammatory bowel diseases such as Crohn's, constipation, diverticulitis, ulcerative colitis and diarrhea.

As a last word on fiber, the longer the fermentation, the higher the levels of organic acids present in the dough. So for anyone who is looking to slow down the rate at which the bread is assimilated, I recommend choosing the retarded method, especially in light of the study conducted by Liljeberg et al. in 1996, that demonstrated significantly increased levels of resistant starch in breads with higher levels of lactic acid.

MANY OF US FAIL TO GET THE RECOMMENDED DAILY INTAKE OF FRUIT AND VEGETABLES, SO BREAD TAKES ON AN EVEN MORE IMPORTANT ROLE AS A POTENTIAL SOURCE OF FIBER

Nutrients, phytonutrients, & phenolic compounds

When it comes to bread, using whole-wheat flour gives us a health advantage because it contains many natural anti-carcinogens. A number of studies show that fiber and certain vitamins, the mineral selenium, and phenolic compounds found in whole grains, reduce potential cancer-causing chemicals in the body.

What is really significant when it comes to sourdough, is that initial studies indicate that fermenting wheat increases the level and bio-accessibility of the phenolic compounds and vitamins found in wheat. Levels of folates and phenolic compounds are almost doubled by the sourdough fermentation process, indicating that sourdough may offer more protection against a range of diseases than yeasted bread.

It is important to understand that the most abundant phenolic compounds found in wheat are the phenolic acids and flavonoids located in the outer layer of the grain. For this reason, every loaf we bake at the School contains some whole-wheat stone-ground flour. These nutritional properties can only be fully exploited by using whole-wheat flour; preferably fresh and stone-ground. In recent years our knowledge of the additional biologically active compounds in the grain has increased significantly. And it is these compounds that are thought to be among the main factors contributing to the protective properties of whole-wheat foods. Although the outer layers of grains contain much higher levels of phytochemicals, such as phenolic acids and folate (vitamin B_{12}), not every loaf I make is 100% whole-wheat, simply because not using white flour would be too limiting. Some just prefer lighter loaves, while others with digestive malaise, I suggest should initially avoid very fiber-rich bread to begin with.

It is the higher levels of acidity that is the key to increased availability of these remarkable compounds. It makes more sense when you realize that most of the phenolic compounds in bran are bound to carbohydrates, and can survive gastrointestinal digestion, reaching the colon intact. It is here in the large intestine that they provide an antioxidant environment.

Long, slow fermentation has also been shown to increase the folate content in the baking process of both wheat and rye flour. (Folate is a B vitamin used as a supplement by women to prevent neural tube defects from developing during pregnancy, and to treat anemia caused by folic acid deficiency.) In particular, the levels of folates in rye fermentation more than doubled according to one study. The content of thiamine, which our bodies use to produce energy, has also been shown to increase when making slow-fermented breads, and there are studies that show retention of riboflavin—needed for growth and overall good health—and vitamin E, mainly present in wheat germ.

SO WHY IS SOURDOUGH MORE BENEFICIAL THAN YEASTED BREAD WHEN IT COMES TO MICRONUTRIENTS?

Minerals are inorganic compounds needed for your body to function properly, and they all come from the same source: the earth. Minerals make their way into plants as they grow in the soil. And we absorb the minerals from the plants that we eat.

Iron deficiency is the most widespread nutrient deficiency in the world, estimated to affect over two billion people. Zinc deficiency is also extensive, particularly in sub-Saharan Africa and South Asia. Wheat is a significant source of both of these minerals. Whole-wheat flour is a good source of vital minerals, including calcium, potassium, magnesium, iron, and zinc. Although whole-wheat bread may contain high levels of these minerals, their absorption by our body may be limited, due to the presence of phytic acid, the principal store of phosphorus in seeds, found in the bran part of wheat. Phytic acid binds with minerals in the digestive tract and so impairs mineral absorption. Consuming just 5–10mg of phytic acid can reduce iron absorption by 50%. Basically, you poop out all the good stuff.

Unlike cows, that have a compartment in their stomach for fermenting grass, we don't have a built-in fermentation to break down the grain. Luckily we have the ability to let our ally, lactic acid bacteria, predigest the grain for us, making it easier for us to absorb the minerals, and fully access the nutritional richness of whole-wheat flours. As sourdough ferments, the lactic acid bacteria produce lactic acid, which in turn activates various enzymes within the whole-wheat flour. One of these enzymes is phytase, which breaks down phytic acid. Certain strains of lactic acid bacteria have also been shown to produce their own phytase enzymes, helping to reduce the amount of phytic acid present by up to 70%, and thereby enabling a large proportion of minerals present within the whole-wheat to be readily accessible and absorbed by our body.

The problem for people with compromised digestive systems is that undigested phytic acid can cause wind. People with IBS can end up feeling very bloated and uncomfortable as the gas extends already sensitive intestines. Anything that neutralizes the phytic acid, such as the slow fermentation of wheat in making sourdough, will reduce bloating and gas, making bread easier to digest for most people with IBS.

There is another element here worth mentioning again—sourdough isn't just easier to digest for people with IBS. Whole-wheat sourdough is also a prebiotic, providing the support and nourishment that helps nourish the often already compromised gut microbes.

Vitamins & minerals in whole-wheat flour

Fermenting whole-wheat flour results in a remarkable nutritional and flavor transformation making the bread not just delicious, but also increasing the bioavailability of most of the vitamins, minerals, and antioxidants in flour.

Vitamins

VITAMIN E is a fat-soluble vitamin that acts as an antioxidant in the body. It is needed for the proper function of many organs, and is associated with naturally slowing aging. Its benefits include treating and preventing diseases of the heart and blood vessels, as well as improving high blood pressure and blocked or hardened arteries.

VITAMIN B_2 (riboflavin) is also a water-soluble vitamin, but it cannot be stored in the body, so we need a daily dose. It has strong antioxidant properties, and is responsible for maintaining healthy blood cells, helping to boost energy levels, facilitating a healthy metabolism, preventing free radical damage, contributing to growth, and protecting skin and eye health. Like all B vitamins, it helps digest and extract energy from the foods we eat, which it does by converting nutrients from carbohydrates, fats, and proteins into useable energy. For this reason, B_2 is needed for the functioning of every single cell within your body.

VITAMIN B_3 (niacin) is another water-soluble vitamin, whose benefits include the ability to reduce and control cholesterol levels. Most diabetics are able to effectively control blood glucose levels with the help of niacin, and it can also reduce their risk of high blood cholesterol and heart disease, which is commonly seen in patients with diabetes.

VITAMIN B_5 (pantothenic acid) has many health benefits, including the alleviation of conditions such as asthma, hair loss, allergies, stress and anxiety, and respiratory disorders. Like the other B vitamins, vitamin B_5 plays a role in energy metabolism. It plays a role in the synthesis of fat, hormones, and carbohydrates that we take in from the foods we eat, turning them into usable energy.

VITAMIN B_6 (pyridoxine) supports brain development and function. Studies show that a vitamin B_6 deficiency contributes to cognitive and memory impairment, Alzheimer's, and dementia. Vitamin B_6 also plays an important role in making the hormones serotonin and norepinephrine, known as the "happy hormones", which help to control mood, energy, and concentration.

VITAMIN B_{12} benefits the central nervous system, helping to maintain the health of nerve cells, including those needed for neurotransmitter signaling. It also helps form the protective covering of nerves known as the myelin sheath. When vitamin B_{12} levels are low, almost every cognitive function can suffer.

VITAMIN K is another fat-soluble vitamin that plays an important role in blood clotting. It is essential for strong bones, helps prevent heart disease, and is crucial for other bodily processes. Recent evidence also suggests vitamin K is an important adjunct to vitamin D.

VITAMIN B$_1$ (thiamine) is a water-soluble vitamin that is used in nearly every cell in the body. It plays an important role in maintaining a healthy nervous system, and improving the cardiovascular functioning of the body. Without high enough levels of thiamine, the molecules found in carbohydrates and proteins cannot be properly used by the body to carry out various important functions.

VITAMIN B$_9$ (folate) is important because it plays a role in DNA synthesis and repair, and encourages cell and tissue growth. It should not be confused with folic acid, a synthetic version used for food fortification and supplements.

CHOLINE is a water-soluble macronutrient that is key for liver function and brain development, nerve function, and muscle movement, supporting energy levels and maintaining a healthy metabolism.

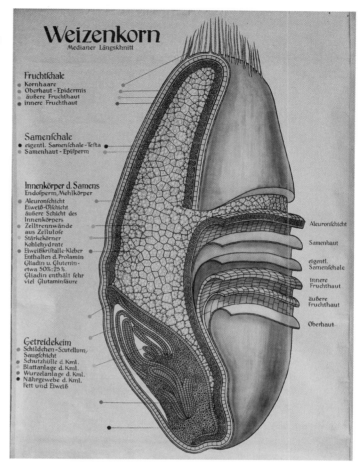

Minerals

CALCIUM is used to build and maintain strong bones. Our heart, muscles, and nerves also need calcium to function properly.

IRON is an important component of hemoglobin, essential for carrying life-giving oxygen to blood cells.

MAGNESIUM helps maintain muscle and nerve function. It keeps heart rhythm steady, supports a healthy immune system, and keeps bones strong. It also helps regulate blood sugar levels, promotes normal blood pressure, and is known to be involved in energy metabolism and protein synthesis.

MANGANESE benefits a healthy bone structure and bone metabolism. It also assists metabolic activity in the human body.

PHOSPHORUS is a vital part of our growth process (it is equally important to plants), and works in association with calcium to create strong bones and teeth.

POTASSIUM can provide relief from stroke, high blood pressure, heart and kidney disorders, anxiety, and stress. It also maintains muscle strength, and keeps the nervous system functioning normally.

SODIUM is an electrolyte that plays an essential part in fluid maintenance within the human body. It also plays a pivotal role in enzyme activity and muscle contraction.

ZINC helps the immune and digestive systems to function optimally.

SELENIUM is an essential trace mineral of fundamental importance to human health as it has positive antiviral effects, is needed for successful male and female fertility and reproduction, and also reduces the risk of cancer, autoimmune, and thyroid diseases.

FODMAPs

One of the things that has become clear to me is that the symptoms of IBS can be easily confused with the symptoms of non-celiac gluten sensitivity. The advice to sufferers who experience persistent or frequent bloating, is that a special diet called the low FODMAP diet can be effective.

FODMAP stands for fermentable oligosaccharides, disaccharides, monosaccharides and polyols. These are types of carbohydrates that are not easily broken down and absorbed by the gut. In patients suffering from IBS, or people who have wheat sensitivity/intolerance, the malabsorption of these sugars is related to the lack of enzymes to fully break down these complex sugars, which results in them being transported untouched into the colon, where they ferment, causing gas. Worryingly, some reasearch indicates that these sugars not only exacerbate IBS, but there are suggestions that they may possibly even cause non-celiac wheat sensitivity.

The good news is that research has shown that the long fermentation process of sourdough bread diminishes the levels of FODMAP carbohydrates by 90%, making sourdough suitable for consumption by IBS sufferers. What I have come to believe, is that a large proportion of people self-diagnosing gluten intolerance, are actually more likely to have IBS, especially when you consider that IBS is the most common functional gastrointestinal (GI) disorder, and worldwide estimates of prevalence range from 10–20%. Often when people cut out wheat, they are actually inadvertently cutting out FODMAPS, and yet gluten somewhat unfairly gets the blame. In recent years a multimillion dollar industry has been built around misunderstanding wheat, and many free-from products are packed full of additives and expensive ingredients that do very little to nourish or support the protective microbes that are integral to good health. Much of the explanation of why sourdough is more digestible for the majority of people, lies in the fact that levels of fructans are drastically reduced during fermentation. Specifically, the enzymes triggered by the acids produce lactic acid bacteria, and get busy breaking down these otherwise non- degradable carbohydrates into food that has been shown to support our gut microbes. The evidence points to the fact that fermenting is not just the key to avoiding the symptoms of IBS, but may well also be the key to both preventing and recovering from IBS.

Lipids & fatty acids

Wheat germ is the small, nutrient-dense center of a wheat kernel. It's only about 2.5% of the weight of the kernel, but is a rich source of B vitamins, proteins, dietary fiber, minerals, and phenolic compounds, as well as being one of the most attractive plant-based protein sources. It also contains a range of beneficial lipids and fatty acids, the most abundant of which is linoleic acid, followed by palmitic and oleic acids. These are the "essential" fatty acids that cannot be synthesized by our bodies, and therefore need to be supplied through diet. They are associated with a range of nutritional and health benefits, such as maintaining cholesterol levels, improving physical endurance, and delaying the effects of aging. Extracting maximum benefits from these unsaturated fatty acids has always been a challenge for food scientists, because of the high lipid-destabilizing enzymes present in wheat germ. These enzymes oxidize the fatty acids, destroying their nutritional and health-promoting benefits. This oxidization has also been attributed to the short shelf life of products containing wheat germ, which is why it is completely removed by the industrial process. However, the long, slow fermentation of sourdough can preserve the nutritional state of wheat germ fatty acids, as it results in lower levels of the oxidizing enzyme lipase, increasing the shelf life. It also increases phytase activity, thereby increasing the bioavailability of minerals.

Bioactive peptides

The lactic acid fermentation of cereals produces bioactive peptides. These are of particular interest because of their anti-inflammatory, anti-diabetic and antioxidant properties. Bioactive peptides are the active components of a protein, which, when they are separated from the protein, act as they would do if they were still attached. Bioactive peptides are rapidly absorbed into our bloodstream, and depending on their function, they then either enter the cell directly, and move to their target site, or they reside on the cell itself, and perform their job on and between the cells. In the dairy industry, there are some well-documented clinical studies that have shown that milk-derived bioactive peptides have health-promoting potential, and they are therefore being targeted at diet-related diseases such as obesity, cardiovascular diseases, and diabetes. Peptides derived from cow, goat, sheep, buffalo and camel milk, have multifunctional properties, including antimicrobial and antioxidant properties. They help regulate immunological, gastrointestinal, hormonal, and neurological responses, and so play a vital role in the prevention of cancer, osteoporosis, hypertension, and other disorders.

Recent laboratory studies have shown that sourdough fermentation results in the production of amounts of bioactive peptides equivalent to those found in the dairy industry. However, the sourdough industry cannot make any claims on these findings, because as yet, no clinical trials have been carried out. However, the findings do show that bioactive peptides survive the baking process, and that they are readily absorbed during digestion.

As well as their potential health benefits, bioactive peptides, and amino acids generated by sourdough fermentation help improve bread quality, taste, flavor, and texture. In fact, bioactive peptides are precursors to aroma and flavor compounds, so you can literally taste the goodness in sourdough.

Lower glycemic index & diabetes

I had been teaching sourdough for a year or so when I began to see a pattern emerging. About one in ten enquiries to the school were from diabetics asking how sourdough fermentation might help to regulate blood sugar. I found a study about fiber-rich sourdough actively retarding starch digestibility leading to low glycemic responses by Terry Graham, Professor in Human Health and Nutritional Sciences at the University of Guelph, Ontario. Professor Graham and his team of researchers had studied four types of breads to determine which had the most positive health benefits in terms of carbohydrate metabolism, blood sugar, and insulin levels. The research, which took place in two studies over seven years, focused on carbohydrate metabolism in humans. He chose bread as a high carbohydrate food to use in his trials. "I rapidly found out that bread is an extremely complex food, and its properties change not only with ingredients, but how it's made, how it's baked, how it's served", Terry explained. The results of the studies showed that the type of grains used, the way they were milled, and how the bread was made, all affected the properties of a loaf—pointing toward stone-ground flour as the most positive. More importantly, the team discovered that the long fermentation of sourdough, resulted in a loaf that was digested more slowly, and caused less of a spike in blood sugar levels.

The team then looked at other hormonal responses, and included other breads in their trials. The results consistently showed sourdough to be associated with more moderate blood sugar response. This is because fermentation alters the way in which starch is digested and assimilated into the body, which means that it acts more slowly, resulting in less pronounced responses in terms of blood glucose and insulin. All of which have positive implications for people trying to control their blood sugar levels.

SO HOW DOES SOURDOUGH CHANGE THE WAY THE BODY ASSIMILATES STARCH?

Firstly, it is through the use of whole grains that contain the starchy endosperm, germ, and bran of the grain. The beneficial health effects of whole grains include the amount and type of fiber present, and the presence of bioactive compounds, which are concentrated in the bran layers of the grain.

It is known that fiber slows down postprandial glucose and insulin responses (the mild decrease in blood sugar after eating a big meal) by having a bulking effect, and presumably taking longer to digest, minimizing blood glucose spikes. But, compared to normal fast-fermented breads, sourdough also contains more resistant starch.

Sourdough bread made with whole-wheat, roller-milled flour was found to show a similar response to white flour, while a sprouted grain sourdough (see page 48) showed the most positive response. Lower insulin levels may also contribute to the protective effects of whole grains. In many people, the risk of atherosclerotic cardiovascular disease, diabetes, and obesity is linked to insulin resistance. Again, higher intakes of whole grains are associated with increased sensitivity to insulin. Why? Because whole grains improve insulin sensitivity by lowering the glycemic index of the diet, while increasing its content of fiber, magnesium and vitamin E.

Breadmaking equipment

There is a huge array of equipment available in shops, and on the internet. Some will help you to get consistently good results in your breadmaking, while others are nice to have, and will make your baking experience more pleasurable. I like to use vintage or handcrafted items, as I love the feel of a hand-carved wooden spoon, or the way a handmade pot feels as I mix. I use the same equipment each time I make bread. Do this, and you will soon become familiar with the way dough rises in your favorite bowl, and how stiff the mixture is as you bring together the flour and water in your starter.

BAKING PARCHMENT Freeform loaves can be given their final proof and then baked on parchment paper sprinkled with semolina—so much easier for moving the risen dough into the oven.

BAKING STONE A baking stone can make all the difference to the bake of your loaves. Preheated for at least half an hour, the stone retains heat, and helps to produce a good crusty base.

BANNETONS These baskets give your sourdough loaf that artisan look, and help to form a nice, chewy crust by wicking moisture away while the dough proofs. Cane bannetons can be used un-lined, and will leave a spiral pattern on the dough, while wicker baskets need a linen liner called a *couche*. They come in different shapes and sizes.

BREAD BIN A bread bin with a lid is ideal for storing soft breads, keeping them fresh for longer.

BREAD BAG A cloth or paper bread bag is perfect for storing crusty bread.

CROCK-POTS WITH LIDS Ideal for keeping your sourdough starter in. It's useful to have two pots: one in use, and one washed out and ready to transfer the starter into when the first one needs a clean.

COUCHE If you're baking regularly, investing in a linen *couche* makes a lot of sense. The cloth provides support to the dough during the second proof, and wicks moisture away to help give a better shape and crust to the finished loaf.

DOUGH SCRAPER A plastic scraper is an inexpensive piece of equipment, but one that makes a huge difference to your baking experience. It makes handling sticky dough during kneading and shaping so much easier. It's also handy for cleaning up the work surface after you have prepared your dough.

DOUGH CUTTER Use a stainless-steel cutter for cleanly dividing dough into portions. Choose one with a handle that will be comfortable to use.

DUTCH OVEN/*LA CLOCHE* This is a covered earthenware or cast-iron baking pot for baking breads. Keep the lid on at the start of the bake to get a good rise before the crust forms.

FLOUR BIN A large storage jar or flour bin with a lid is useful for keeping flour dry and free of dirt.

FLOUR SIFTER This saves having to put a dough-covered hand into the bag of flour when dusting your work surface while kneading. I like to have two sifters or pots—one with flour for dusting the work surface, and another with semolina for sprinkling into bannetons.

KITCHEN TIMER It's all too easy to forget that your dough needs folding, or a loaf in the oven should be checked. A good timer is invaluable as a prompt to get back to the kitchen.

LAME* OR *GRIGNETTE Essentially a razor blade with a handle, this is used to score the dough before baking, allowing you to control the rise of each loaf. Choose one with a replaceable blade, and keep it sharp at all times so it cuts rather than tears the dough.

LOAF PANS A heavy-duty, non-stick loaf pan will turn out perfect loaves every time. Having a couple of pans of different sizes adds to the variety of loaves you can bake.

MEASURING CUPS Some formulas call for cup measures, so it's good to have a set on hand.

MEASURING PITCHER A glass measuring pitcher is useful for mixing hot and cold water to get the temperature right for mixing dough.

MEASURING SPOONS These are useful for measuring salt, as well as seeds, herbs, and other additions to the dough.

LARGE MIXING BOWL I have a beautiful vintage, stoneware mixing bowl. A good large bowl gives you plenty of space to make dough without ending up with flour all over the work surface and floor, so it is better to choose a bowl that's bigger than you think you'll need.

SMALL MIXING BOWL Useful for mixing *levains* to leave overnight for the next day's dough.

NOTEBOOK I like to keep records of everything from measurements, temperatures, and timings to the results of each bake. This helps me learn, eliminate mistakes, and produce even better bread next time around. A small notebook keeps all this information in one place and easy to find.

OVEN MITTS Essential for taking hot loaves from the oven, and if pans need turning partly through baking to insure an even bake.

PEEL Use a flat tool to slide loaves into the oven smoothly and quickly, reducing the chance of bumping your nicely risen dough, and keeping heat loss from the oven to a minimum.

PULLMAN PAN This is a square-sided pan used to bake loaves that are perfect for sandwich making.

SCALE An accurate food scale is a must for consistent results. Digital scales are easy to use, and usually go up in increments of 1g—ideal for weighing small amounts of yeast and salt. There are scales that allow you to weigh in baker's percentages, cutting out the need for calculations when you want to change formula proportions.

SPRAY BOTTLE Adding steam to the oven as you put a loaf in to bake allows the crust to remain soft, and to expand, giving a better rise. An easy way to get steam in a domestic oven, is to spray the interior using a bottle sold for spraying plants, before quickly closing the door.

TEMPERATURE PROBE A metal spike with a thermometer on one end. Use it to check the internal temperature of your loaves to insure a perfect bake.

THERMOMETER Temperature has a huge impact on fermentation, and can be controlled in a number of ways. Insure the water you use to make the dough is at the right temperature using a basic thermometer.

WIRE RACK A rack for cooling baked loaves is essential—it doesn't need to be anything fancy; the same one you use for cooling home- baked cakes is perfect.

WOODEN SPOONS I love using hand-carved, robust heavy spoons —not only to support other artisans, but because good spoons feel amazing in your hand.

DISH TOWELS A damp dish towel can be used to cover your mixing bowl during bulk proofing; used clean and dry, it can be sprinkled with semolina to stand in for a *couche* for proofing loaves shaped as batons and baguettes.

Essential equipment

A LARGE BOWL
A DOUGH SCRAPER
A WHISK
A *LAME*
2 X 1KG LINED BANNETONS OR A 16-INCH LENGTH OF *COUCHE* (OR HEAVY DUTY COTTON DISH TOWELS)
A *LA CLOCHE* BAKING DOME OR A DUTCH OVEN

Resources

ONLINE

Being a sourdough baker often goes hand in hand with being part of a community. Social media is an open community, which gives us an opportunity to exchange ideas with bakers across the world. While I appreciate that some people are cautious about using social media, it really is up to you as to how much you engage—sometimes it's great just to dip in and read.

The Sourdough Club All students who attend a course at The Sourdough School become a member of our own community of bakers. Everyone else can subscribe and join this online resource. We provide videos, instructions, detailed information, and support to inspire and encourage club members in their breadmaking. Follow us on Instagram (@sourdoughclub), and find us at The Sourdough Club on Facebook .

www.facebook.com/groups/perfect-sourdough Perfect Sourdough is a Facebook group run by Teresa Greenway. A brilliant resource, and a great forum for sharing, with over 40,000 members at this point.

My favourite community is on Instagram. Most of the bakers and millers listed are friends and colleagues, they are also a great resource for ideas and inspiration, and I love browsing through the beautiful photos they post.

@alicequillet Alice is a wonderful baker, determinedly showing up the French and making really great bread and coffee—co-owner of Ten Belles in Paris.

@boncipane Bonci Gabriele is a good friend who bakes brilliant pannetone and pizza.

@campbell2664 A creator of baking equipment and fabulous bread.

@ceorbread Guy Frenkel is a baker from Los Angeles, posting beautiful photos of his bread.

@danlepard Dan has mentored me for almost a decade. He is amazing, and is well-known for his baking and writing. Without Dan I wouldn't be teaching.

@emsbread Emmanuel Hadjiandreou is a dear friend, award-winning baker, author, and Sourdough School tutor.

@gilchesters Farmers and millers in the north east of England growing organic, heritage grains.

@illebrod Norwegian baker with principles, and Sourdough School tutor Martin Fjeld.

@katesbread Kate Pepper is a Californian baker who posts inspiring photos of her work.

@maurizio Maurizio Leo is a sourdough baker and writer at theperfectloaf.com

@michaeljames77 Baker, author, and owner of the Tivoli Road Bakery.

@mjjtightlines Matthew is a really great friend, and just an amazing baker. His bread is divine, and he bakes at Outerlands in San Francisco

@mulinomarino Photos from my favourite Italian mill, and long-time friends.

@richardhartbaker Based in Copenhagen, Richard is the most instinctive and brilliant baker I have ever met—one of the best in the world.

@season_adam Adam is a tutor at the School, and baked all the bread in the photos of this book. He is a fantastic sourdough baker with a superb technical and practical knowledge of sourdough.

@smallfoodbakery Photos from one of the most inspiring women and bakers I know—Kimberley Bell.

@sourdoughschool Lots of photos of bread and events here at the School.

@vanessakimbell My own account, with plenty of pictures of the breads I bake.

@white_crystals I love Crystal White. An incredible baker, she is based in San Diego, California.

@yohanferrant Half French, half Spanish, meet my friend and extraordinary baker in Spain.

INGREDIENTS AND EQUIPMENT

www.sourdough.co.uk I sell much of the baking equipment that we use at the School through our website. All the flours I use are also available through the shop pages of the website.

www.bakerybits.co.uk I'm a huge fan of this website, especially as I wrote the newsletter and developed the formulas for five years. It's an amazing resource for everything related to breadmaking.

www.preservedgoods.com Crock pots and starters are available from this site.

FLOUR

I personally know each and every miller listed below, in the UK, Italy, France and the USA. I have stood in the fields, and chatted to the farmers who grow the grain they mill into the flour I make the bread with at the School. I believe this connection between farmers, bakers, and producers is integral to understanding your main ingredient and key to making great bread, so I'd encourage everyone who makes sourdough, to try to get to know the millers and farmers involved in growing and milling their flour.

www.mulinomarino.it My favorite Italian mill. I've used them for more than seven years and their Organic type "00" and "0" are the main bread flours I've used throughout this book. A gorgeous family, and such amazing farmers who are deeply connected to their land and community.

www.foricher.com A French mill, which produces the superb organic T65 flour. Ethical, passionate, seventh-generation millers.

www.centralmilling.com American millers, deeply passionate about flavor, the environment and their relationship with their growers. I use their organic artisan baker's craft (ABC) flour, which is milled from a carefully selected blend of organic wheat.

www.flour.co.uk Marriage's is another superb supplier of organic bread flour. Highly recommended, especially for blending.

www.dovesfarm.co.uk Doves Farm produces fantastic rye flour, and it's the one I've used in formulas throughout this book. Their bread flour is also superb.

www.gilchesters.com British-grown, organic flours, milled from heritage wheat varieties. The whole-wheat flour has been used throughout this book. The organic whole-wheat is fantastically flavorsome and perhaps my favorite flour—I blend it into virtually every loaf I make. Andrew and Billie are great friends, and have incredible milling and flour knowledge.

www.priorsflour.co.uk My local mill. Highly recommended. Local wheat milled in my local mill by amazing miller and friend Jonathan Cook.

I also highly recommend the **Lammas Fayre heritage flours** produced by archeobotanist and heritage grain pioneer John Letts, who also tutors at the School. These flours are milled from ancient cereal varieties, grown using traditional methods. Again, I have used them throughout the formulas and they are available to buy from Bakery Bits Ltd.

Extensive research was completed to write this book, however, there is not room to list the hundreds of studies used. For those interested, all source material and references listed are linked to the original studies at sourdough.co.uk.

Index

a

acetic acid 18, 21, 23
acidity 21, 61, 192
agriculture 26–9, 58, 184
alcohol, "hooch" 64, 65
allergies 186, 187, 188
amaranth, sprouting 49
ambient method 70
    adding salt 98
    leaven 91
    proofing dough 104
    shaping loaf 101
amino acids 39, 48, 187, 188, 198
amylase 18, 35, 127
autoimmune diseases 186, 189
autolyze 42, 96–7

b

bacteria: in soil 10, 23, 26, 58, 189
    see also lactic acid bacteria
baguettes, sourdough 176–81
baking 110–11
bannetons 102
barley 33
    cracked black barley and
    stout bread 174–5
bassinage 42, 98
batards 102
    beet, black pepper, and
    feta batards 148
beer: cracked black barley and
    stout bread 174–5
    see also spent beer malted
    grains
beets: beet and black
    pepper starter 46
    beet, black pepper and
    feta batards 148
bioactive peptides 198
blackberry, poppy seed, and
    pea flower water bread 130–1
black currant and fennel
    starter 45
bloating 193

blood sugar levels 199
boules 102
    classic 50:50 whole-wheat/
    white sourdough boule 119
    classic white sourdough
    boules 114
    classic whole-wheat
    sourdough boules 120–123
    malted muesli boule 171
    ramson boules 133–5
    seeded sourdough boules 129
    soy, ginger, and rice
    sourdough boules 161
    whole-wheat sourdough
    boules 120–3
    yogurt light spelt boules 167
bran 36, 38, 192, 193, 199
buckwheat 33
bulk fermentation 99
butter: butter spice paste 146
    herb butter 133–5
butterfly pea tea 130
buttermilk sourdough,
    Scandinavian 141
    butyrate 190

c

cacao: chocolate and roast
    hazelnut bread 144–5
calcium 193, 195
calcium carbonate 36, 38
Canadian flour 42
Candida milleri (humilis) 22, 26
carbohydrates 196, 199
carbon dioxide (CO_2) 18, 21, 58
charcoal 45
cheese: beet, black pepper,
    and feta batards 148
    jalapeño and cheese loaf 137
cherries (sour): smoked
    kibbled rye and wild cherry
    sourdough 154

chocolate: chocolate and roast
    hazelnut bread 144–5
    chocolate starter 46, 61, 85
cholesterol 196
choline 195
classic 50:50 whole-wheat/
    white
    sourdough boule 119
classic sourdough (higher
    hydration) 116
classic white sourdough
    boules 114
classic whole-wheat
    sourdough
    boules 123
cloches 110
Clostridium botulinum 21
coatings 102
celiac disease 186, 187, 189
cornmeal (maize, polenta):
    jalapeño and cheese loaf 137
    pumpkin and polenta
    sourdough 162
cracked black barley and stout
    bread 174–5
Crohn's disease 189, 191

d

dextrose 61
diabetes 189, 190–1, 199
diastatic malt 51
digestive problems 186, 191
disaccharides 186, 196
dough: adding salt 98
    autolyze 96–7
    bulk fermentation 99
    mixing 94–5
    proofing 104
    readiness to bake 107
    resting 101
    scoring 108–9
    shaping loaf 100–3
drying starter 45–6

durum wheat 33, 42
    100% heritage sourdough
    in a pan 124
durum wheat semolina:
    tomato and herb bread 140
Dutch ovens 110

e

E. coli 21
Earl Grey, fig, and kamut®
    loaf 151
eau de bassinage 98
einkorn 33
    100% heritage sourdough in
    a pan 124
    einkorn and spent ale grain
    sourdough 172
    Scandinavian buttermilk
    sourdough 141
emmer 34
    100% heritage sourdough in
    a pan 124
    Scandinavian buttermilk
    sourdough 141
enzymes 18, 21, 35, 120, 193, 196
equipment 200–1
essential fatty acids 196
esters 18, 65
ethanol 18
exopolysaccharides 21, 61

f

farming 26–9, 58, 184
fatty acids 196
fermentation 10
    autolyze 96–7
    bulk fermentation 99
    and enzymes 120
    modern bread 184
    speed of 35
    starter 58
fermented rosewater 142
fiber 38, 186, 189, 190–1, 196, 199

Index

Acknowledgements

The first person to thank is my incredible husband. Without his belief in me, constant help, support, and deep love, the School would never have been built, and I wouldn't be writing this book. I cannot find words that express my feelings, but you and me sitting in a tree is close. To my family, who have all been so understanding and so patient—my gorgeous son, William, who helps in classes at the school, as does my youngest daughter, Isobel, who is always willing to help out, and delights me with her love total love of bread, and my amazing eldest daughter, Libiana, for the countless suppers she has made supporting me while I've had my head down writing. Thank you—without your help we'd all have starved to death! My parents, too, have given me constant support, without which I just couldn't have done this.

A huge thank you to microbiologist and miller Stefan Cappelle, and baker and musician Karl De Smedt at Puratos for their constant support and for giving me access to their incredible resources.

Thank you to my team. Lucy Jennings, my PA, whose unwavering support keeps me together —you are amazing. Sarah Smith, who is forever untangling my words and helping me support my students. And Dr. Amrita Vijay for her research, and for guiding me through the complexities of the science of digestion—Amrita, you are fabulous. And my friend Bran Sugden, for his hard work and friendship, helping me to tend the fruits and vegetables in the garden. There are also literally hundreds of students to thank, too many to name, but particular thanks to Phil Jones.

Thank you to my agent Michael Alcock—chin up. Thank you to Adam Pagor for putting the formulas through their paces, and creating the breads that feature in the photographs.

To both Vicky Orchard and Judith Hannam, my editors. I don't think anyone else could have picked out the knowledge and structured it so beautifully; so brilliantly. A huge thanks also to Isabel Gonzalez-Prendergast. Thanks too to Helen Bratby for the simple, yet brilliantly innovative book design. Nassima Rothacker for the beautiful photographs, and Ashley Lovejoy Hart. To the wonderful Kyle Cathie, who has supported me at every step. A massive thank you to Patrick Thornberry from Bakery Bits for his constant support and friendship. Thank you to Emmanuel Hadjiandreou, and to E.J. Ozborne of Hatchet and Bear for the amazing tools & hands, and likewise to Barry. Thank you also to David Whitehouse for giving me a proper kick up the butt when it was most needed, and to Matthew J. Jones for sharing his thoughts. And lastly, my deepest thanks to Richard Hart, whose philosophy that bread has the power to to transform, educate, inspire, and motivate has inspired all around him, including me, to bake with passion and conviction.